St. Joseph
MILLENNIUM
PRAYER BOOK

May the Jubilee Year 2000
be a time of grace and blessing
for you and your family.

With prayerful gratitude
for your service to our parish family.

The Church asks all Catholics to celebrate the Millennium with fervent prayer and meditation on the Incarnation and the Redemption carried out by the Triune God.

St. Joseph
MILLENNIUM
PRAYER BOOK

CONTAINING A MULTITUDE OF PRAYERS
IN ACCORD WITH THE THEMES
EMPHASIZED BY THE CHURCH
FOR THE GREAT JUBILEE
OF THE YEAR 2000

Illustrated

CATHOLIC BOOK PUBLISHING CO.
New Jersey

NIHIL OBSTAT: Francis J. McAree, S.T.D.
Censor Librorum

IMPRIMATUR: ✠Patrick J. Sheridan, D.D.
Vicar General, Archdiocese of New York

Acknowledgments: Litanies (pp. 26-29) and the "Prayer To Imitate Mary in Receiving God's Word" (p. 39) are taken from *Celebrations for the Millennium: 1997* © 1997, Catholic Book Publishing Co. (CBPC); "Come, Holy Spirit" (p. 33), "Consoler Spirit" (p. 34), "Intercessions for the Spirit" (p. 35), "Invocations to the Holy Spirit" (p. 36), and "Mysteries of the Rosary" (p. 41) are taken from *Celebrations for the Millennium: 1998* © 1997, CBPC; "Praise for the Creator" (p. 21) and "The Father's Saving Plan" (p. 22) are taken from the *Sacramentary* © 1985, International Committee on English in the Liturgy (initial capitals added); "Te Deum" (p. 20) and *"Magnificat"* (p. 40) are taken from *Prayers We Have in Common* © 1975, International Consultation on Church Texts (initial capitals added); Acts of Love (p. 23), Faith (p. 29), and Hope (p. 36) are taken from *St. Joseph Baltimore Catechism* © 1962, CBPC.

(T-930)

4

CONTENTS

FOREWORD

The Church has called upon all Catholics to celebrate the Millennium of the Year 2000 in a spirit of prayer and meditation on the wondrous works of the Incarnation and the Redemption. She has especially asked us to remember the themes of God the Creator, God the Redeemer, and God the Sanctifier.

This book of prayers is drawn up to help us in this task. It puts at our fingertips ready-made prayers, a precious treasury of words by which we can approach God every day and at the same time dwell on the themes of the Millennium.

Some of the prayers are taken from the Church's Liturgy and are what may be termed *official*. Others are taken from the Church's living Tradition, including the wide repertory of prayers composed by Saints and holy Popes. Still others come from the life-situation of Catholics throughout the ages.

Prayers of this type also convey a deeper knowledge and understanding of the Church's teaching. In a subtle and unobtrusive fashion they teach the Faith while allowing us to approach God. By using them, we not only get closer to God but also come to know Him better with every passing day.

It goes without saying that we can also pray in our own words instead of words found on a printed page—and indeed we must do so. However ready-made prayers are there for those times when we do not know what to say and need help in speaking to God. We need the help of past ages as well as present trends to say what we feel and what we should feel.

The prayers presented herein deal with many of the most important concerns of life. They can be used with full confidence that they will help us celebrate the Millennium in the best way possible.

At times, the prayers do not speak to God but of God. Yet they are so filled with His presence that they become true prayers for us. Such prayers call upon our brothers and sisters in the Faith, other people in general, and all creation to adore, thank, and praise God.

Some prayers make use of the plural "us" instead of the singular "me." The reason is obvious: each believer (whether he or she knows it or not) always prays with the whole Church and in the name of the Church.

Every effort has been made to ensure that this book will be easy to use and attractive to the person praying. The text is printed in large pleasing typeface and in red and black. The inspiring colorful illustrations will help keep our minds on the Divine Persons of the Blessed Trinity.

May all who use this prayerbook celebrate the Millennium in the way desired by the Church and achieve a deeper and more vital spiritual life. May it lead them ever closer to the eternal union with the living God.

PREPARING FOR THE THIRD MILLENNIUM

A Time of Salvation

On November 14, 1994, Pope John Paul II issued an apostolic letter entitled *Tertio Millennio Adveniente* ("As the Third Millennium Draws Near").

The letter succinctly expresses the essential connotation of the category of "time" and its fundamental importance in Christianity. For human beings are not indifferent to the passage of time; they contemplate interiorly the unfolding of the History of Salvation.

Within the dimension of time the world was created, within it the History of Salvation unfolds, finding its culmination in the "fullness of time" of the Incarnation and its goal in the glorious Return of the Son of God at the end of time. In Jesus Christ, the Word made flesh, time becomes a dimension of God, Who is Himself eternal.

With the coming of Christ there begin "the last days" (cf. Heb 1:2), the "last hour" (cf. 1 Jn 2:18) and the time of the Church, which will last until the Parousia (no. 10).

Hence, Christ's words and actions during the earthly existence are not reproduced anew, but insofar as they are actions of the Incarnate Word they are actual and efficacious saving actions for those who celebrate them. The solar year is permeated by the Liturgical Year, which in a certain way reproduces the whole mystery of the Incarnation and Redemption, beginning from the First Sunday of Advent and ending on the Solemnity of Christ the King (no. 10).

Indeed, as Pius XII declared, the Liturgical Year "is not a cold and lifeless representation of the events of the past nor a simple and bare record of a former age. It is rather Christ Himself Who is ever living in His Church. Here He continues that journey of immense mercy that He lovingly began in His mortal life, going about doing good, with the design of bringing human beings to know His Mysteries and in a certain way live by them" (*Mediator Dei*, no. 165).

The Custom of Jubilees

John Paul II reminds us that in the Old Testament the jubilee was a time dedicated in a special way to God. It fell every seventh year, according to the Mosaic Law: this was the sabbatical year, during which the earth was left fallow and slaves were set free. In this year, in addition to the freeing of slaves, the Law also provided for the cancellation of all debts in accordance with precise regulations. And this was to be done in honor of God.

What was true for the sabbatical year was also true for the jubilee year, which fell every 50 years. In the jubilee year, however, the customs of the sabbatical year were broadened and celebrated with even greater solemnity. On this occasion every Israelite regained possession of his ancestral land if he happened to have sold it or lost it by falling into slavery. He could never be completely deprived of it because it belonged to God. Nor could the Israelites remain forever in a state of slavery, since God had redeemed them for Himself as His exclusive possession by freeing them from slavery in Egypt (no. 12).

The prescriptions for the jubilee year largely remained ideals—more a hope than an actual fact. They thus foretold the freedom that would be won by the coming Messiah. They led to a kind of social doctrine that emerged more clearly in the New Testament. The jubilee year was meant to restore equality among all the children of Israel, offering new possibilities to families that had lost their property and even their personal freedom.

On the other hand, the jubilee year was a reminder to the rich that a time would come when their Israelite slaves would once again become their equals and would be able to reclaim their rights (no. 13).

For the Church, the jubilee is a year of the Lord's favor, a year of the remission of sins and of the punishments due to them, a year of reconciliation between disputing parties, a year of manifold conversions and extrasacramental penance. The tradition of jubilee years involves the granting of indulgences on a larger scale than at other times.

Together with jubilees recalling the mystery of the Incarnation, at intervals of 100, 50, and 25 years, there are also jubilees that commemorate the event of the Redemption: the Cross of Christ, His Death on Calvary, and the Resurrection. On these occasions, the Church proclaims a year of the Lord's favor, and she tries to ensure that all the faithful can benefit from this grace (no. 14).

The Great Jubilee of 2000: A New Advent

Since all jubilees refer to the salvific dimension of "time," they point to the Messianic mission of Christ, Who came as the One anointed by the Holy Spirit, the One sent by the Father. It is He Who proclaims the Good News to the poor. It is He Who brings liberty to those deprived of it, Who frees the oppressed and gives back sight to the blind.

He ushers in a year of the Lord's favor, which He proclaims not only with His words but above all with His actions. The jubilee, a year of the Lord's favor, characterizes all the activity of Jesus; it is not merely the recurrence of an anniversary in time (no. 11).

Thus the jubilee of the year 2000 is a proclamation of a year of the Lord's favor. It expresses both the internal and the external joy of the Church for salvation; the 2000 years from the birth of Christ represent an extraordinarily *great jubilee* not only for Christians but indirectly for the whole of humanity, given the prominent role played by Christianity during these two millennia (no. 15).

The proximate preparation for this jubilee was providentially initiated with the Second

Vatican Council, a council focused on the Mystery of Christ and His Church and at the same time open to the world (no. 18). This great assembly, humbly heeding the Word of God, reaffirmed the universal call to holiness, and made provision for the reform of the Liturgy, the "origin and summit" of the Church's life (no. 19).

This jubilee is a new Advent for the life of the Church (nos. 20-23): "The yearly Advent Liturgy is the season nearest to the spirit of the Council. For Advent prepares us to meet the One Who was, Who is, and Who is to come" (cf. Rv 4:8) (no. 20).

The Council opened the journey—abundantly explicitated in the present pontificate—of preparation for the year 2000, whose basic theme is the new evangelization (no. 21).

In this preparation the particular Churches have also had a large part (no. 25) as have the Eastern Churches, whose ancient patriarchates are so closely linked to the apostolic heritage and whose venerable theological, liturgical, and spiritual traditions constitute a tremendous wealth that is the common patrimony of the whole of Christianity (no. 25).

First Phase: 1994-1996

The whole immediate preparation was oriented toward the celebration of the Mystery of Christ the Savior (nos. 30ff).

The first phase (1994-1996) was of an ante-preparatory character. It was meant to revive in the Christian people an awareness of the value and meaning of the Jubilee of the Year 2000 in human history. As a commemoration of the birth of Christ, the jubilee is deeply charged with Christological significance (no. 31).

Once again there appear the specific notes of celebration, articulated in conformity with the Christian Faith in Word and Sacrament. The structure of the memorial is linked with that of celebration, not limiting commemoration of the event only to ideas but also making its saving significance present through the celebration of the Sacraments (no. 31).

The Jubilee of the Year 2000 is meant to be a great prayer of praise and thanksgiving, especially for the gift of the Incarnation of the Son of God and of the Redemption that He accomplished (no. 32). However, the joy of this jubilee is always in a particular way a joy based on the forgiveness of sins, a joy of conversion, emphasizing anew the theme of the Synod of Bishops of 1983: penance and reconciliation (no. 32) and pointing to the sins that have been detrimental to the unity willed by God for His people (nos. 34, 50).

There should also be an examination of conscience concerning the reception given to the Council, this great gift of the Spirit to the Church at the end of the second millennium. Some of the questions to be asked are the following.

To what extent has the Word of God become more fully the soul of theology and the inspiration of the whole of Christian living as *Dei*

Verbum sought? In addition, is the Liturgy lived as the origin and summit of ecclesial life, in accordance with the teaching of *Sacrosanctum Concilium*? And is the ecclesiology of communion described in *Lumen Gentium* being strengthened in the Universal Church and in the particular churches? (no. 36).

Second Phase—Year 1

The second phase (1997-1999) is the properly preparatory one. It is structured as a three-year period, centered on Christ, the Son of God made Man and is thus Trinitarian.

The first year, 1997, will be devoted to reflection on Christ, the Word of God, made Man by the power of the Holy Spirit. The distinctly Christological character of the jubilee needs to be emphasized, for it will celebrate the Incarnation and coming into the world of the Son of God, the Mystery of salvation for all humankind. The general theme proposed for this year is: "Jesus Christ, the one Savior of the world, yesterday, today, and forever" (cf. Heb 13:8) (no. 40).

In order to recognize Who Christ truly is, Christians, especially in the course of this year, should turn with renewed interest to the Bible, "whether it be through the Liturgy, rich in the Divine Word, or through devotional reading, or through instructions suitable for the purpose and other aids" (*Dei Verbum*, 25) (no. 40).

The letter goes on to recommend that the Mystery of salvation be made sacramentally present and a renewed appreciation of Baptism as the basis of Christian living be obtained (no. 41). At the same time it invokes a revitalized Ecumenism as another conducting thread of the jubilee both within and without the Church (nos. 6, 25, 34, 41, 47, 53, 55, 56).

The Blessed Virgin, who will be as it were indirectly present in the whole preparatory phase, will be contemplated in this first year especially in the mystery of her Divine Motherhood. It was in her womb that the Word became flesh! The affirmation of the central place of Christ cannot therefore be separated from the recognition of the role played by His holy Mother (no. 43).

Veneration of Mary, when properly understood, can in no way take away from "the dignity and efficacy of Christ the one Mediator" (*Lumen Gentium*, 62). Mary, in fact, constantly points to her Divine Son and she is proposed to all believers as the model of faith that is put into practice (no. 43).

Second Phase—Year 2

The second year, 1998, will be dedicated in a particular way to the Holy Spirit and to His sanctifying presence within the community of Christ's disciples. For the Mystery of the Incarnation was accomplished "by the power of the Holy Spirit." It was brought about by that Spirit—consubstantial with the Father and the Son—Who, in the absolute Mystery of the tri-une God, is the Person-Love, the uncreated

Gift, Who is the eternal source of every gift that comes from God in the order of creation, the direct principle and, in a certain sense, the subject of God's self-communication in the order of grace. The Mystery of the Incarnation constitutes the climax of this giving, His Divine self-communication (no. 44).

The Spirit makes present in the Church of every time and place the unique revelation brought by Christ to humanity, making it alive and active in the soul of each individual. In this sense, the Liturgy is the continual gift of the Holy Spirit to bring about communion. That is why the Liturgy takes place "in the unity of the Holy Spirit."

Hence the primary tasks of the preparation for the jubilee include a renewed appreciation of the presence and activity of the Spirit, Who acts within the Church both in the Sacraments, especially in Confirmation, and in the variety of charisms, roles, and ministries that He inspires for the good of the Church (no. 45).

Mary, who conceived the Incarnate Word by the power of the Holy Spirit and then in the whole of her life allowed herself to be guided by his interior activity, will be contemplated and imitated during this year as the woman who was docile to the voice of the Spirit, a woman of hope and a radiant model of trust in God's promises (no. 48).

Second Phase—Year 3

The final year of preparation, 1999, will be aimed at broadening the horizons of believers so that they will see things in the perspective of Christ: in the perspective of the "Father Who is in heaven" (cf. Mt 5:45), from Whom the Lord was sent and to Whom He has returned (cf. Jn 16:28).

The whole of the Christian life is like a great pilgrimage to the house of the Father, Whose unconditional love for every human creature, and in particular for the "prodigal son" (cf. Lk 15:11-32), we discover anew each day. The jubilee, centered on the person of Christ, thus becomes a great act of praise to the Father (no. 49).

The Liturgy is the expression of theology, that is, of the confession of the wonders worked by God the Father in salvation history. In relation to the very celebration of the jubilee, the apostolic letter desires to give a particular emphasis to the celebrative phase, since its object is the glorification of the Trinity from Whom everything in the world and in history comes and to whom everything returns (no. 55).

In the perspective of the History of Salvation, the Liturgy is always a Divine gift to the Church and a work of the Holy Trinity. The Trinitarian dimension of worship is a fundamental theological principle of its nature and the primary law of every celebration.

Mary most holy, the highly favored daughter of the Father, will appear before the eyes of believers as the perfect model of love toward both God and neighbor (no. 54).

OFFICIAL PRAYERS OF THE CHURCH

Praying with the official prayers of the Church for the Millennium is one of the best ways to keep in our minds the themes for this extraordinary event. In this way, we will prepare for and live the Great Jubilee of the Year 2000.

During the period leading up to and through the Third Millennium and the Great Jubilee of the Year 2000, the Church recommends that we focus on prayers that concern the Mystery of Salvation, specifically Christ the Redeemer (and faith), the Holy Spirit, the Sanctifier (and hope), and God the Father, Lord and Creator (and love) as well as the Blessed Virgin Mary, Mother of God.

While the remaining sections in this book reproduce approved prayers related to these themes, *this section provides* official prayers concerning those same themes, *which are found in one or other service book of the Church, e.g.,* Celebrations for the Millennium. *Judicious use of these prayers will enable us to keep the themes firmly rooted in our minds and to act on them whenever possible.*

In this way, we will take our rightful place in the celebration of the Great Jubilee, which is meant to be a prayer of praise and thanksgiving, especially for the gift of the Incarnation of the Son of God and of the Redemption that He accomplished. We will also be mindful that the joy of the Jubilee is always in a particular way a joy based on the forgiveness of sins, a joy of conversion, emphasizing anew the theme of penance and reconciliation.

In addition, use of these prayers will ensure that we will live the final years of this century in a deepened spirit of Advent that will prepare us for the Third Millennium and that we will live the Millennium itself in the same spirit so as to be ready for the eternal Millennium in heaven.

PRAYERS TO GOD THE FATHER

The Te Deum

You are God: we praise You;
You are the Lord: we acclaim You;
You are the eternal Father:
All creation worships You.

To You all Angels, all the Powers of heaven,
Cherubim and Seraphim, sing in endless
praise:
    Holy, holy, holy, Lord, God of power and
    might,
    heaven and earth are full of Your glory.

The glorious company of Apostles praise You.
The noble fellowship of Prophets praise You.
The white-robed army of Martyrs praise You.

Throughout the world the holy Church ac-
claims You:
    Father, of majesty unbounded,
    Your true and only Son, worthy of all worship,
    and the Holy Spirit, advocate and guide.

You, Christ, are the King of glory,
the eternal Son of the Father.

When You became Man to set us free
You did not spurn the Virgin's womb.

You overcame the sting of death,
and opened the Kingdom of heaven to all believers.

You are seated at God's right hand in glory.
We believe that You will come, and be our
Judge.

Come then, Lord, and help Your people,
bought with the price of Your own Blood,
and bring us with Your Saints
to glory everlasting.

℣. Save Your people, Lord, and bless Your inheritance.

℟. *Govern and uphold them now and always.*

℣. Day by day we bless You.

℟. *We praise Your Name for ever.*

℣. Keep us today, Lord, from all sin.

℟. *Have mercy on us, Lord, have mercy.*

℣. Lord, show us Your love and mercy;

℟. *for we put our trust in You.*

℣. In You, Lord, is our hope:

℟. *and we shall never hope in vain.*

Praise for the Creator

Father in heaven,
it is right that we should give You thanks and glory:
You are the one God, living and true.
Through all eternity You live in unapproachable light.
Source of life and goodness, You have created all things,
to fill Your creatures with every blessing
and lead all men to the joyful vision of Your light.
Countless hosts of Angels stand before You to do Your Will;
they look upon Your splendor

and praise You, night and day.
United with them,
and in the name of every creature under
heaven,
we too praise Your glory as we sing (say):

Holy, holy, holy Lord, God of power and might,
heaven and earth are full of Your glory.
Hosanna in the highest.
Blessed is He Who comes in the Name of the
Lord.
Hosanna in the highest.

The Father's Saving Plan

Father, we acknowledge Your greatness:
all Your actions show Your wisdom and love.
You formed man in Your own likeness
and set him over the whole world
to serve You, his Creator,
and to rule over all creatures.
Even when he disobeyed You and lost Your
friendship
You did not abandon him to the power of
death,
but helped all men to seek and find You.
Again and again You offered a Covenant to
man,
and through the Prophets taught him to hope
for salvation.
Father, You so loved the world
that in the fullness of time You sent Your only
Son to be our Savior.

He was conceived through the power of the
    Holy Spirit,
and born of the Virgin Mary,
a Man like us in all things but sin.
To the poor He proclaimed the Good News of
    salvation,
to prisoners, freedom,
and to those in sorrow, joy.
In fulfillment of Your Will
He gave Himself up to death;
but by rising from the dead,
He destroyed death and restored life.
And that we might live no longer for ourselves
    but for Him,
He sent the Holy Spirit from You, Father,
as His first gift to those who believe,
to complete His work on earth
and bring us the fullness of grace.

An Act of Love

O my God,
I love You above all things,
with my whole heart and soul,
because You are all-good and worthy of all
    love.
I love my neighbor as myself
for the love of You.
I forgive all who have injured me,
and ask pardon of all whom I have injured.

PRAYERS TO JESUS THE REDEEMER

Prayer To Be Ready for the Millennium

Lord Jesus, Lord of History,
Who came at the fullness of time,
prepare our hearts to celebrate with faith
the great Jubilee of the Year 2000,
that it may be a year of grace and mercy.
Give us a heart that is humble and simple,
a heart that can contemplate
the Mystery of the Incarnation
with an ever increasing wonder,
for You, Son of the Most High,
have become our Brother
in the womb of the Virgin Mary,
temple of the Holy Spirit.

℟. *Glory and praise to You, Lord Jesus Christ,
today and forever!*

Jesus, origin and fulfillment of the new man,
turn our hearts to You,
that we may abandon the paths of error
and walk in Your footsteps
on the road that leads to life.
Enable us to live our faith fully
according to the promises we made at Baptism,
and that we may be fearless witnesses of Your
    Word,
so that the life-giving light of the Gospel
may shine forth in our families and in society. ℟.

Jesus, power and wisdom of God,
create in us love for the Holy Scriptures,
where the voice of God the Father can be heard,

the voice that enlightens and inflames,
that nourishes and consoles.
Voice of the Living God,
renew the missionary thrust of the Church,
so that all nations may come to know You,
true Son of God and Son of Man,
the one Mediator between God and man. ℟.

Jesus, source of unity and peace,
strengthen the bonds of unity within Your
      Church;
intensify the activity of the ecumenical move-
      ment
so that all Your disciples,
through the power of the Holy Spirit,
may all be one.
You Who have given us as a rule of life
the new commandment of love,
transform us into builders of an interdepen-
      dent world,
where war will give way to peace
and the culture of death to a commitment to
      life. ℟.

Jesus, only Son of the Father,
full of grace and truth,
Light that enlightens all men,
give Your life in abundance
to all who seek You with a sincere heart.
To You, Redeemer of mankind,
the beginning and the end of time and of the
      universe;
to the Father,

inexhaustible source of all good;
and to the Holy Spirit, seal of infinite love,
all honor and glory forever and ever. R℣.

John Paul II

Litany of the History of Salvation

Lord, have mercy.
Christ, have mercy.
Lord, have mercy.

Christ, hear us.
Christ, graciously hear us.

Father in heaven,
R℣. *have mercy on us.*

Son, Redeemer of the world,
R℣.

Holy Spirit, the Paraclete,
R℣.

Holy Trinity, one God, R℣.

Jesus, beloved Son of the Father,
Divine Wisdom,
splendor of His glory, R℣.

Jesus, son of Adam,
descendant of Abraham,
holy seed of David, R℣.

Jesus, fulfillment of prophecy,
fullness of the Law,
destiny of human beings,
R℣.

Jesus, gift of the Father,
conceived by the power of the Spirit,
Son of the Virgin Mary,
R℣.

Jesus, born for our salvation,

revealed to shepherds,
manifested to the magi,
R℣.

Jesus, light of the gentiles,
glory of Israel,
expectation of the nations, R℣.

Jesus, baptized in the Jordan,
consecrated by the Spirit,
sent by the Father, R℣.

Jesus, tempted in the desert,
praying on the mountain,
glorious on Tabor, R℣.

Jesus, teacher of truth,
Word of life,
way to the Father, R℣.

Jesus, healer of the sick,
consolation of the afflicted,
mercy of sinners, R℣.

Jesus, way and gate of salvation,
Shepherd and Lamb,
resurrection and life, R℣.

Jesus, condemned to death,
crowned with thorns,
covered with wounds, R℣.

Jesus, nailed to the wood,
entombed in the earth,
raised from the dead, R℣.

Jesus, descended into hell,
 ascended into heaven,
 giver of the Spirit, ℟.

Jesus, longed for by the
 Spouse,
 prize of the Just,
 fullness of the Kingdom,
 ℟.

To You, O Jesus, the Living
 One, *glory and praise.*

To You, O Jesus, living in
 the Church, *glory and
 praise.*

To You, O Jesus, living for-
 evermore, *glory and
 praise.*

Litany of Jesus, God and Man

Lord, have mercy.
Christ, have mercy.
Lord, have mercy.

Christ, hear us.
Christ, graciously hear us.

Father in heaven,
 ℟. *have mercy on us.*
Son, Redeemer of the world,
 ℟.
Holy Spirit, the Paraclete,
 ℟.
Holy Trinity, one God, ℟.

Jesus, true God, Son of the
 Father,
Jesus, true Man, born of
 Mary,
Jesus, Redeemer of the
 world,
Jesus, Messiah and Savior,
 ℟. *praise and glory to You.*

Uncreated beauty,
Divine Wisdom,
Life without end,
Sure hope, ℟.

Jesus, Light from eternal
 Light,

Jesus, radiant Morning
 Star,
Jesus, dawn of the new
 man,
Jesus, day without sunset,
 ℟.

Glory of the Patriarchs,
Fullness of the Law,
Fulfillment of the prophe-
 cies,
Author of the new Cove-
 nant, ℟.

Christ, living Word of the
 Father,
Christ, revealer of the
 Father,
Christ, announcer of the
 Good News,
Christ, Prophet of the King-
 dom, ℟.

Divine Teacher,
High Priest,
King of glory,
Only Mediator, ℟.

Jesus, gentle and humble
Jesus, true Holy One,

Jesus, faithful witness
Jesus, lamb and shepherd,
℟. *praise and glory to You.*

Our brother and friend,
Our guide and advocate,
Our journey and goal,
Our peace and rest, ℟.

Lord of glory, crucified,
Lord, risen from the dead,
Lord, ascended to the Father's right hand,
Lord, giver of the Spirit, ℟.

Divine Passover,
Passover of the New Covenant,
Passover of the Church
Eternal Passover, ℟.

Jesus, God-with-us,
Jesus, spouse of the Church,
Jesus, ineffable presence,
Jesus, everlasting joy, ℟.

Jesus, the first and the last,
Jesus, Lord of history,
Jesus, universal Judge,
Jesus, living and coming, ℟.

Lamb of God, You take away the sins of the world; *have mercy on us.*

Lamb of God, You take away the sins of the world; *have mercy on us.*

Lamb of God, You take away the sins of the world; *have mercy on us.*

Litany of Jesus Our Redeemer

Lord, have mercy.
Christ, have mercy.
Lord, have mercy.

Christ, hear us.
Christ, graciously hear us.

Father in heaven,
℟. *have mercy on us.*
Son, Redeemer of the world, ℟.

Holy Spirit, the Paraclete, ℟.

Holy Trinity, one God, ℟.

Jesus, Holy One of God,
Jesus, the only Just One,
Jesus, obedient Son,
Jesus, face of the Divine mercy,
℟. *give us Your salvation.*
Redeemer of humanity,

Savior of the world,
Victor over death,
Strong and victorious prince, ℟.

Jesus, Servant of the Lord,
Jesus, Man of Sorrows,
Jesus, united with the poor,
Jesus, kind to sinners, ℟.

Christ, our reconciliation,
Christ, our life,
Christ, our hope,
Christ, our peace and harmony, ℟.

Jesus, word that saves,
Jesus, hand stretched out to sinners,
Jesus, way that leads to peace,
Jesus, light that conquers the darkness, ℟.

Jesus, sustainer of the weak,

Jesus, peace of the oppressed,

Jesus, comfort of the suffering,

Jesus, mercy of sinners, ℞.

Jesus, defense of the offended,

Jesus, welcome of the excluded,

Jesus, justice of the oppressed,

Jesus, homeland of the exiled, ℞.

Heart of Christ, pierced by a lance,

Heart of Christ, victim of expiation,

Heart of Christ, rich in mercy,

Heart of Christ, fount of holiness, ℞.

Blood of Christ, price of our ransom,

Blood of Christ, poured out for our sins,

Blood of Christ, seal of the New Covenant,

Blood of Christ, drink and purifying bath, ℞.

Jesus, Lamb of God,

Jesus, Lamb without blemish,

Jesus, Redeeming Lamb,

Jesus, Victorious Lamb, ℞.

Jesus, gate of the city of peace,

Jesus, firstborn of the new creation,

Jesus, lamp of the eternal Jerusalem,

Jesus, guardian of the book of life, ℞.

Lord, from You springs forth the water of life,

Lord, from You flows the redeeming Blood,

Lord, through You the Holy Spirit is given to us,

Lord, through You paradise is reopened, ℞.

Lamb of God, You take away the sins of the world; *have mercy on us.*

Lamb of God, You take away the sins of the world; *have mercy on us.*

Lamb of God, You take away the sins of the world; *have mercy on us.*

An Act of Faith

O my God,
I firmly believe that You are
one God in three Divine Persons,
Father, Son, and Holy Spirit;

I believe that Your Divine Son became Man,
and died for our sins,
and that He will come to judge the living and
    the dead.
I believe these and all the truths
which the Holy Catholic Church teaches
because You have revealed them,
Who can neither deceive nor be deceived.

PRAYERS TO THE HOLY SPIRIT

Prayer for the Millennium

Holy Spirit,
most welcome guest of our hearts,
reveal to us the profound meaning
of the Great Jubilee
and prepare our hearts
to celebrate it with faith,
in the hope that does not disappoint,
in the love that seeks nothing in return.
Spirit of truth,
You Who search the depths of God,
Memory and Prophecy in the Church,
lead human beings to recognize in Jesus of
    Nazareth
the Lord of glory,
the Savior of the world,
the supreme fulfillment of history.

℞. *Come, Spirit of love and peace!*

Creator Spirit,
hidden builder of the Kingdom,
by the power of Your Saints
guide the Church
to cross with courage the threshold
of the New Millennium
and to carry to the coming generations
the light of the Word
Who brings salvation.
Spirit of holiness,
Divine Breath Which moves the universe,
come and renew the face of the earth.
Awaken in Christians
a desire for full unity,
that they may be for the world
an effective sign and instrument
of intimate union with God
and of the unity of the whole human race.

℟. *Come, Spirit of love and peace!*

Spirit of communion,
soul and strength of the Church,
grant that the wealth of charisms
and ministries
may contribute to the unity
of the Body of Christ,
and that the laity, consecrated persons,
and ordained ministers
may work together in harmony
to build the one Kingdom of God.
Spirit of consolation,
unfailing source of joy and peace,

inspire solidarity with the poor,
grant the sick the strength they need,
pour out trust and hope
upon those experiencing trials,
awaken in all hearts
a commitment to a better future.

℟. *Come, Spirit of love and peace!*

Spirit of wisdom,
inspiration of minds and hearts
direct science and technology
to the service of life, justice, and peace.
Render fruitful our dialogue
with the followers of other religions,
lead the different cultures
to appreciate the values of the Gospel.
Spirit of life,
by Whose power the Word was made flesh
in the womb of the Virgin Mary,
the Woman of attentive silence,
make us obedient to the promptings
of Your love
and ever ready to accept
the signs of the times
that You place along the paths of history.

℟. *Come, Spirit of love and peace!*

To You, Spirit of love,
with the Almighty Father
and the only-begotten Son,
be praise, honor, and glory,
forever and ever.   John Paul II

Come, Holy Spirit

Come, Holy Spirit, come!
And from Your celestial home
Shed a ray of light Divine!

Come, Father of the poor!
Come, source of all our store!
Come, within our bosoms shine!

You, of comforters the best;
You, the soul's most welcome guest;
Sweet refreshment here below;

In our labor, rest most sweet;
Grateful coolness in the heat;
Solace in the midst of woe.

O most blessed Light Divine,
Shine within these hearts of Yours,
And our inmost being fill!

Where You are not, man has naught,
Nothing good in deed or thought,
Nothing free from taint of ill.

Heal our wounds, our strength renew;
On our dryness pour Your dew;
Wash the stains of guilt away:

Bend the stubborn heart and will;
Melt the frozen, warm the chill;
Guide the steps that go astray.

On the faithful, who adore
And confess You, evermore
In Your sev'nfold gift descend;

Give them virtue's sure reward;
Give them Your salvation, Lord;
Give them joys that never end.

Consoler Spirit

Heavenly King, Consoler Spirit, Spirit of Truth,
present everywhere and filling all things,
treasure of all good and source of all life,
come dwell in us, cleanse and save us,
You Who are All-Good.

Come, Holy Spirit, Creator Blest

Come, Holy Spirit, Creator blest,
And in our souls take up Your rest;
Come with Your grace and heavenly aid
To fill the hearts which You have made.

O Comforter, to You we cry,
O heavenly gift of God Most High,
O fount of life and fire of love,
And sweet anointing from above.

You in Your sevenfold gifts are known;
You, finger of God's hand we own;
You, promise of the Father, You
Who do the tongue with power imbue.

Kindle our senses from above,
And make our hearts o'erflow with love;
With patience firm and virtue high
The weakness of our flesh supply.

Far from us drive the foe we dread,
And grant us Your peace instead;
So shall we not, with You for guide,
Turn from the path of life aside.

Oh, may Your grace on us bestow
The Father and the Son to know;
And You, through endless times confessed,
Of both the eternal Spirit blest.

Now to the Father and the Son,
Who rose from death, be glory given,
With You, O holy Comforter,
Henceforth by all in earth and heaven.

Intercessions for the Spirit

Lord Jesus
You have promised and given to Your Church
the Spirit Counselor;
confirm in those who believe and hope in You
the gift of the Holy Spirit:

℟. *Send forth Your Spirit, O Lord, and renew
the face of the earth.*

In Your Spirit, give wisdom to our hearts. ℟.

In Your Spirit, give understanding to our
minds. ℟.

In Your Spirit, give us counsel in our uncer-
tainties. ℟.

In Your Spirit, give us fortitude in our weak-
nesses. ℟.

In Your Spirit, give true knowledge to our
thought. ℟.

In Your Spirit, give us piety in our intentions.
In Your Spirit, give us fear of the Lord in our
　　lives. ℟.
In Your Spirit, give us strength in our weak-
　　nesses. ℟.
In Your Spirit, give us faith in our prayer. ℟.
In Your Spirit, give us hope for our journey. ℟.
In Your Spirit, give charity to our actions. ℟.

Invocations to the Holy Spirit

L et us invoke the Holy Spirit, acclaiming:

℟. *Come and give us Your counsel!*

Holy Spirit, voice of the Prophets. ℟.
Holy Spirit, sweet whisper Divine. ℟.
Holy Spirit, guide to the truth. ℟.
Holy Spirit, interior master. ℟.
Holy Spirit, breath of life. ℟.
Holy Spirit, inspirer of holiness. ℟.
Holy Spirit, living reminder of the Gospel. ℟.

An Act of Hope

O my God,
relying on Your almighty power
and infinite mercy and promises,
I hope to obtain pardon for my sins,
the help of Your grace,
and life everlasting,
through the merits of Jesus Christ,
my Lord and Redeemer.

PRAYERS TO THE BLESSED VIRGIN MARY

Prayer to Mary for Help in Preparing for the Millennium

We greet you, Daughter of God the Father!
We greet you, Mother of the Son of God!
We greet you, Spouse of the Holy Spirit!
We greet you, dwelling-place of the Most Holy
    Trinity!
With this greeting we come before you
[on your feast day]
with the trust of children. . . .

Abide with us, Immaculate Mother,
in the heart of our preparation
for the Great Jubilee of the Year 2000.
We beseech you, watch especially over the
    triduum,
formed of the last three years of the second
    millennium,
1997, 1998, and 1999,
years dedicated to contemplation
of the Trinitarian Mystery of God.
We would like this eventful century of ours
and the second Christian millennium
to close with the seal of the Trinity.
It is in the Name of the Father, and of the Son
    and of the Holy Spirit
that we begin our daily work and prayer.

It is in turning again to the heavenly Father
that we end our activities by praying:
"Through our Lord Jesus Christ, Your Son,
Who lives and reigns with You, in the unity of
the Holy Spirit."
Thus, in the sign of the Trinitarian Mystery,
the Church in Rome, united with believers
throughout the world,
approaches in prayer the end of the 20th century,
to enter the Third Millennium with a renewed
heart.

We greet you, Mother of the Son of God!
We greet you, Spouse of the Holy Spirit!
We greet you, dwelling-place of the Most Holy
Trinity!
This greeting highlights
how deeply you are imbued with God's own
life,
with His profound and ineffable Mystery.
You have been totally imbued with this Mys-
tery
from the first moment of your conception.
You are full of grace; you are immaculate!

We greet you, Immaculate Mother of God!
Accept our prayers and, as Mother, deign to
bring the Church
in Rome and throughout the world
into that fullness of time
toward which the universe has been advancing

since the day Your Divine Son,
our Lord Jesus Christ
came into the world.
He is the beginning and the End, the Alpha
   and the Omega,
the King of the ages, the First-born of all creation,
the First and the Last.
In Him all is definitely fulfilled;
in Him, every reality grows to the full stature
   desired by God
in His mysterious plan of love.

We greet you, Virgin most prudent!
We greet you, Mother most clement!
Pray for us,
intercede for us,
Immaculate Virgin,
our merciful and powerful Mother,
Mary!   John Paul II

Prayer To Imitate Mary in Receiving God's Word

Lord, our God,
You have made the Virgin Mary
the model of those who receive Your Word
and put it into practice.
Hear our supplications
and with the power of Your Spirit
grant that we too may become a holy place
in which your Word of salvation is carried out.

Mother of Hope

O Immaculate Virgin,
permit us,
all of us who carry in our hearts
the experiences and wounds of the twentieth
    century,
now nearing its end,
to approach the inestimable gift [of peace]
which Christ has offered us by being born of
    you,
two thousand years ago!
Permit us to enter into the fast approaching
    Third Millennium
filled with hope!

John Paul II

The Magnificat

My soul proclaims the greatness of the Lord,
my spirit rejoices in God my Savior
for He has looked with favor on His lowly ser-
    vant.

From this day all generations will call me
    blessed:
the Almighty has done great things for me,
and holy is His Name.

He has mercy on those who fear Him
in every generation.

He has shown the strength of his arm,
He has scattered the proud in their conceit.

He has cast down the mighty from their
    thrones,
and has lifted up the lowly.

He has filled the hungry with good things,
and the rich He has sent away empty.

He has come to the help of His servant Israel
for He has remembered His promise of mercy,
the promise He made to our fathers,
to Abraham and his children for ever.

Mysteries of the Rosary

*Five Mysteries of the lives of the Lord Jesus and the
Blessed Virgin Mary are proposed for prayerful meditation. In these Mysteries the action of the Holy Spirit is
especially evident.*

*The format consists of: the announcement of the Mys-
tery, a brief scriptural text, a moment of silence, the Our
Father, ten Hail Marys, the Glory to the Father, and a
concluding prayer. The Hail Mary may also be recited in
the following way: the first part of the Hail Mary may be
extended with a phrase relevant to the Mystery. The second part, Holy Mary . . . , is only recited at the end of the
ten Hail Marys.*

The First Mystery

The Power of the Holy Spirit Overshadows the Virgin of Nazareth

Scriptural Reading

From the Gospel of Luke   1:28-35
Upon arriving, the Angel said to [Mary]: "Re-
    joice, O highly favored daughter!
The Lord is with you. Blessed are you among
    women."

She was deeply troubled by his words,
and wondered what his greeting meant.
The Angel went on to say to her: "Do not fear,
Mary.
You have found favor with God.
You shall conceive and bear a Son and give
Him the Name Jesus.
Great will be His dignity and He will be called
Son of the Most High.
The Lord God will give Him the throne of
David His father.
He will rule over the house of Jacob forever
and His reign will be without end."
Mary said to the Angel, "How can this be since
I do not know man?"
The Angel answered her: "The Holy Spirit will
come upon You
and the power of the Most High will over-
shadow You;
hence, the holy offspring to be born will be
called Son of God."

The Lord's Prayer

Our Father. . . .

The Hail Mary

Hail Mary, full of grace, the Lord is with you.
Blessed are you among women and blessed is
the fruit of your womb, Jesus,
conceived by the power of the Holy Spirit

(ten times).

Holy Mary, Mother of God,
pray for us sinners now and at the hour of our
death. Amen (the tenth time only).

Glory to the Father

Glory to the Father, and to the Son, and to the
Holy Spirit:

As it was in the beginning, is now, and will be
for ever. Amen.

Prayer

O God,

You chose that at the message of an Angel
Your Word should take flesh
in the womb of the Blessed Virgin Mary.

Grant that we who believe that she is the
Mother of God

may receive the help of her prayers.

We ask this through Christ our Lord.

The Second Mystery

Elizabeth, Filled with the Holy Spirit, Praises the Mother of the Lord

Scriptural Reading

From the Gospel of Luke   1:39-45

Thereupon Mary set out, proceeding in haste
into the hill country to a town of Judah,

where she entered Zechariah's house and
greeted Elizabeth.

When Elizabeth heard Mary's greeting, the
baby leapt in her womb.

Elizabeth was filled with the Holy Spirit and
cried out in a loud voice:

"Blest are you among women and blest is the
fruit of your womb.

But who am I that the mother of my Lord
should come to me?

The moment your greeting sounded in my ears,
the baby leapt in my womb for joy.
Blest is she who trusted that the Lord's words
to her would be fulfilled."

The Lord's Prayer

Our Father. . . .

The Hail Mary

Hail Mary, full of grace, the Lord is with you.
Blessed are you among women and blessed is
the fruit of your womb, Jesus,
bearer of the Spirit of holiness (ten times).

Holy Mary, Mother of God,
pray for us sinners now and at the hour of our
death. Amen (the tenth time only).

Glory to the Father

Glory to the Father, and to the Son, and to the
Holy Spirit:
As it was in the beginning, is now, and will be
for ever. Amen.

Prayer

Lord our God,
Savior of the human family,
You brought salvation and joy
to the home of Elizabeth
through the visit of the Blessed Virgin Mary,
the ark of the New Covenant.
We ask that, in obedience
to the inspiration of the Holy Spirit,
we too may bring Christ to others
and proclaim Your greatness
by the praise of our lips

and the holiness of our lives.
We ask this through Christ our Lord.

The Third Mystery

The Spiritual Maternity of the Virgin Mary at the Foot of the Cross

Scriptural Reading

From the Gospel of John   19:25-30

Near the Cross of Jesus there stood His
    Mother, His Mother's sister,
Mary the wife of Clopas, and Mary Magdalene.
Seeing His Mother there with the disciple
    whom He loved,
Jesus said to His Mother, "Woman, there is
    your son."
In turn He said to the disciple, "There is your
    Mother."
From that hour onward, the disciple took her
    into his care.
After that, Jesus, realizing that everything was
    now finished,
said to fulfill the Scripture, "I am thirsty."
There was a jar there, full of common wine.
They stuck a sponge soaked in this wine on
    some hyssop
and raised it to His lips.
When Jesus took the wine, He said, "Now it is
    finished."
Then He bowed His head, and delivered over
    His spirit.

The Lord's Prayer

Our Father. . . .

The Hail Mary

Hail Mary, full of grace, the Lord is with you.
Blessed are you among women and blessed is
     the fruit of your womb, Jesus,
Who died for our salvation (ten times).

Holy Mary, Mother of God,
pray for us sinners now and at the hour of our
     death. Amen (the tenth time only).

Glory to the Father

Glory to the Father, and to the Son, and to the
     Holy Spirit:
As it was in the beginning, is now, and will be
     for ever. Amen.

Prayer

All-holy Father,
You chose the Easter Mystery
as the way of our salvation;
grant that we, whom Jesus entrusted from the
     Cross
to His Virgin Mother,
may be numbered among Your adopted children.
We ask this through Christ our Lord.

The Fourth Mystery

The Holy Spirit Descends on the Virgin Mary and the Apostles

Scriptural Reading

From the Acts of the Apostles   1:12-14
After [Jesus had been taken up into heaven,]
[the Apostles] returned to Jerusalem from the
     mount called Olivet near Jerusalem

—a mere sabbath's journey away.

Entering the city,

they went to the upper room where they were
    staying:

Peter and John and James and Andrew;

Philip and Thomas, Bartholomew and Matthew;

James son of Alphaeus; Simon, the Zealot
    party member, and Judas son of James.

Together they devoted themselves to constant
    prayer.

There were some women in their company,

and Mary the Mother of Jesus, and His brothers.

The Lord's Prayer

Our Father. . . .

The Hail Mary

Hail Mary, full of grace, the Lord is with you.

Blessed are you among women and blessed is
    the fruit of your womb, Jesus,

inexhaustible source of the Holy Spirit

(ten times).

Holy Mary, Mother of God,

pray for us sinners now and at the hour of our
    death. Amen (the tenth time only).

Glory to the Father

Glory to the Father, and to the Son, and to the
    Holy Spirit:

As it was in the beginning, is now, and will be
    for ever. Amen.

Prayer

Lord our God,
as the Blessed Virgin was at prayer with the
        Apostles
You poured out on her in abundance
the gifts of the Holy Spirit;
grant through her intercession
that we too, being filled with the same Spirit,
may persevere with one mind in prayer
and bring to the world around us
the Good News of salvation.
We ask this through Christ our Lord.

The Fifth Mystery

The Spirit of the Son of God, Born of a Woman, Works in Our Hearts

Scriptural Reading

From the letter of Paul to the Galatians   4:4-7
When the designated time had come,
God sent forth His Son born of a woman, born
        under the Law,
to deliver from the Law those who were sub-
        jected to it,
so that we might receive our status as adopted
        sons.
The proof that you are sons
is the fact that God sent forth into our hearts
        the spirit of His Son
which cries out, "Abba!" ("Father!")
You are no longer a slave but a son!
And the fact that you are a son makes you an
        heir, by God's design.

The Lord's Prayer

Our Father. . . .

The Hail Mary

Hail Mary, full of grace, the Lord is with you.
Blessed are you among women and blessed is
the fruit of your womb, Jesus,
firstborn of the children of God (ten times).

Holy Mary, Mother of God,
pray for us sinners now and at the hour of our
death. Amen (the tenth time only).

Glory to the Father

Glory to the Father, and to the Son, and to the
Holy Spirit:
As it was in the beginning, is now, and will be
for ever. Amen.

Prayer

All-holy Father,
in the wonders of Your wisdom and love
You decreed that Your Son should be born of a
woman,
and be subject to her guidance;
grant that we may enter more and more
into the Mystery of Your incarnate Word
and with Him lead a hidden life on earth
until, escorted by His Virgin Mother,
we may joyously enter
Your home in heaven.
We ask this through Christ our Lord.

THE TRINITY—ONE GOD IN
THREE PERSONS

Our prayer life should manifest the fact that the Blessed Trinity constitutes the central reality for Christians. Our entire lives are lived in the loving embrace of Father, Son, and Holy Spirit.

*T*he Mystery of the Blessed Trinity constitutes the central doctrine of the Catholic Church. A Christian's entire life is marked "in the Name of the Father, and of the Son, and of the Holy Spirit." All life begins in the Trinity and is destined to end in the Trinity.

God has been pleased to reveal this Mystery to us: "In His goodness and wisdom, God chose to reveal Himself and to make known to us the hidden purpose of His Will by which through Christ, the Word made flesh, we have access to the Father in the Holy Spirit and come to share in the Divine Nature" (Vatican II: Constitution on Divine Revelation, *no. 2).*

There are three distinct Persons in one God— and they exist only in relation to one another. They are coequal, coeternal, and consubstantial. The Son proceeds from the Father by generation, and the Holy Spirit proceeds from the Father and the Son by spiration.

God the Father is the Creator, God the Son is the Redeemer, and God the Holy Spirit is the Sanctifier—but not in such a way that the Son and the Holy Spirit are excluded from creation, or the Father and the Holy Spirit from redemption, or the Father and the Son from sanctification.

All of us want to know about God. But it is more important for us to know God, the way two beloved know one another—as the result of an intimate person-to person relationship. The prayers found in this section are intended to help us attain such a knowledge of the three Persons of the Trinity.

(We might point out that, besides the special prayers found in this section, we can also make use of any of the prayers to the Blessed Trinity in the section "Official Prayers of the Church," pp. 18-36.)

Prayer of Consecration to the Trinity

O Everlasting and Triune God,
I consecrate myself wholly to You today.
Let all my days offer You ceaseless praise,
my hands move to the rhythm of Your impulses,
my feet be swift in Your service,
my voice sing constantly of You,
my lips proclaim Your message,
my eyes perceive You everywhere,
and my ears be attuned to Your inspirations.
May my intellect be filled with Your wisdom,
my will be moved by Your beauty,
my heart be enraptured with Your love,
and my soul be flooded with Your grace.
Grant that every action of mine be done
for Your greater glory
and the advancement of my salvation.

Prayer in Praise of the Trinity

I venerate and glorify You,
O most Blessed Trinity,
in union with that ineffable glory
with which God the Father,
in His omnipotence,
honors the Holy Spirit forever.

I magnify and bless You,
O most Blessed Trinity,
in union with that most reverent glory
with which God the Son,
in His unsearchable wisdom,
glorifies the Father and the Holy Spirit forever.

I adore and extol You,
O most Blessed Trinity,
in union with that most adequate and befitting
    glory
with which the Holy Spirit,
in His unchangeable goodness,
extols the Father and the Son forever.

The Glory Be

Glory to the Father,
and to the Son,
and to the Holy Spirit.
As it was in the beginning,
is now, and will be forever.

Litany of the Most Holy Trinity

(For Private Devotion)

Lord, have mercy.
Christ, have mercy.
Lord, have mercy.
Blessed Trinity, hear us.
Adorable Unity, graciously hear us.
God the Father of heaven, *have mercy on us.*
God the Son, Redeemer of the world,*
God the Holy Spirit,
Holy Trinity, one God,
Father, from Whom are all things,
Son, through Whom are all things,
Holy Spirit, in Whom are all things,
Holy and undivided Trinity,
Father everlasting,

* *Have mercy on us* is repeated after each invocation.

Only-begotten Son of the Father,*

Spirit, Who proceed from the Father and the Son,

Coeternal Majesty of Three Divine Persons,

Father the Creator,

Son the Redeemer,

Holy Spirit the Comforter,

Holy, holy, holy Lord God of hosts,

Who are, Who were, and Who are to come,

God, Most High, Who inhabit eternity,

To Whom alone are due all honor and glory,

Who alone do great wonders,

Power infinite,

Wisdom incomprehensible,

Love unspeakable,

Be merciful,
spare us, O Holy Trinity.

Be merciful,
graciously hear us, O Holy Trinity.

From all evil, *deliver us, O Holy Trinity.*

From all sin,**

From all pride,

From all love of riches,

From all uncleanness,

From all sloth,

From all inordinate affection,

From all envy and malice,

From all anger and impatience,

From every thought, word, and deed, contrary to Your holy law,

From Your everlasting malediction,

Through Your almighty power,

Through Your plenteous loving-kindness,

Through the exceeding treasures of Your goodness and love,

Through the depths of Your wisdom and knowledge,

Through all Your ineffable perfections,

We sinners,
we beseech You, hear us.

That we may ever serve You alone,***

That we may worship You in spirit and in truth,

That we may love You with all our heart, with all our soul, and with all our strength,

That, for Your sake, we may love our neighbor as ourselves,

That we may faithfully keep Your holy commandments,

That we may never defile our bodies and our souls with sin,

*Have mercy on us is repeated after each invocation.
**Deliver us, O Holy Trinity is repeated after each invocation.
***We beseech you, hear us is repeated after each invocation.

That we may go from grace
to grace, and from virtue
to virtue,
That we may finally enjoy
the sight of You in glory,
That You would hear us,
O blessed Trinity,
we beseech You, deliver us.
O blessed Trinity,
we beseech You, save us.
O blessed Trinity,

have mercy on us.
Lord, have mercy.
Christ, have mercy.
Lord, have mercy.
℣. Blessed are You, O
Lord, in the firmament of
heaven.
℟. *And worthy to be
praised, and glorious, and
highly exalted forever.*

Let us pray.
Almighty and everlasting God,
You have given us Your servants
grace by the profession of the true Faith
to acknowledge the glory of the eternal Trinity
and in the power of Your Divine Majesty
to worship the Unity.
We beg You to grant that,
by our fidelity in this same Faith,
we may always be defended from all dangers.

Prayer To Be Conformed
to the Divine Will

Most holy Trinity,
Godhead indivisible,
Father, Son, and Holy Spirit,
our first beginning and our last end,
You have made us
in accord with Your own image and likeness.
Grant that all the thoughts of our minds,
all the words of our tongues,

all the affections of our hearts,
and all the actions of our being
may always be conformed to Your holy Will.
Thus, after we have seen here below in appear-
    ances
and in a dark manner by means of faith,
we may come at last to contemplate You
face-to-face
in the perfect possession of You
forever in heaven.

Prayer To Seek God Continually

O Lord my God,
I believe in You,
Father, Son, and Holy Spirit. . . .
Insofar as I can,
insofar as You have given me the power,
I have sought You.
I became weary and I labored.

O Lord my God,
my sole hope,
help me to believe
and never to cease seeking You.
Grant that I may always and ardently
seek out Your countenance.
Give me the strength to seek You,
for You help me to find You
and You have more and more given me
the hope of finding You.

Here I am before You
with my firmness and my infirmity.

Preserve the first and heal the second.

Here I am before You
with my strength and my ignorance.
Where You have opened the door to me,
welcome me at the entrance;
where You have closed the door to me,
open to my cry;
enable me to remember You,
to understand You,
and to love You. St. Augustine of Hippo

Prayer To Live in Union with the Trinity

Omnipotence of the Father,
help my weakness
and save me from the depths of misery.
Wisdom of the Son,
direct all my thoughts, words, and deeds.
Love of the Holy Spirit,
be the source
of all the activity of my mind,
that it may be conformed to the Divine Will.

Doxology to the Blessed Trinity

Holy God, Holy Strong One,
Holy Immortal One, have mercy on us.
To You be praise,
to You be glory,
to You be thanksgiving
through endless ages,
O Blessed Trinity.

GOD THE FATHER—OUR CREATOR
AND LORD

God the Father is our Creator and Lord as well as our loving Father. Prayer to Him enables us to balance His supreme perfections and transcendence with His loving concern for the slightest thing He has made.

Traditionally, God the Father is known as the first Person of the Blessed Trinity. He is truly Father as He begets a coeternal and coequal Son, to Whom He imparts the fullness of His nature and in Whom He contemplates His own perfect image.

By nature God is our Creator and Lord, and we are His creatures and subjects. As a result of sin, however, we have become His enemies and deserve His chastisements. Yet, through the grace of Christ, the Father lovingly pardons us, adopts us as His children, and destines us to share in the life and beatitude of that same Christ, His only-begotten Son.

Thus, by Divine adoption God is our Father and we are His children. This adoption is effected through sanctifying grace, a Divine quality or supernatural habit infused into the soul by God, which blossoms into the vision of glory in eternal life.

Catholics have a tendency to address all prayer to the Father's august Majesty even when they do not name Him directly. In the New Testament, the word "God" as naming someone always means the heavenly Father. Liturgical prayer is almost always addressed to the Father through the Son in the Holy Spirit. By such prayer we acknowledge the presence of the Spirit inspiring us to pray and we also acknowledge that our prayer would be valueless except for the love the Father has for His eternal Son.

(We might point out that, besides the special prayers found in this section, we can also make

*use of any of the prayers to God the Father in the
section "Official Prayers of the Church," pp. 20-
23.)*

Litany of Thanks to God the Father

O my God, You have created me,
and redeemed me by Your beloved Son.
* I thank You with all my heart.
O my God, You have bestowed on me
the Christian Faith
and adopted me as Your child
on the day of my Baptism.*
O my God, You have surrounded me
with so many means of salvation.*
O my God, You have given me
a wonderful Angel to protect me.*
O my God, You have given me a sound intelli-
     gence,
a just judgment, and a loving heart.*
O my God, You have given me eyes that see,
ears that hear, a tongue that speaks,
and limbs that move.*
O my God, You have created
the beautiful sun to give me light,
the waters to refresh me,
and flowers to delight me with their fra-
     grance.*
O my God, You make fruits and crops to ripen,
and increase the animals to nourish and clothe
     us.*
For all the benefits that You will give me
up to my death:*

For the grace of final perseverance,
which I hope to receive from Your mercy
through the merits of Jesus Christ:*
For the infinite happiness
with which You will crown me in heaven
as You have commanded me to hope:*

Prayer of Confidence in the Father's Love

Our Father,
in You we live and move and have our being.
Each day You show us a Father's love.
Your Holy Spirit, dwelling within us,
gives us on earth
the hope of unending joy.

I believe Your gift of the Spirit,
Who raised Jesus from the dead,
is the foretaste and promise
of the Paschal Feast of heaven.

You have taught me to overcome my sins
by prayer, the Sacraments, and good works.
When I am discouraged by my weakness,
give me confidence in Your love.
Let Your compassion fill me with hope
and bring me Your forgiveness, protection, and
    life.

I put my trust in Your love for me.
I know You will never let me be disappointed.

Prayer of Praise

We praise You,
invisible Father,
giver of immortality,
and source of life and light.
You love all human beings,
especially the poor.
You seek reconciliation with all of them
and You draw them to Yourself
by sending Your beloved Son to visit them.

Make us really alive
by giving us the light to know You,
the only true God,
and Jesus Christ Whom You have sent.
Grant us the Holy Spirit
and enable us to speak volumes
about Your ineffable Mysteries. St. Serapion of Thmuis

Prayer of Petition to the Father

Father of mercies,
from Whom comes all that is good,
1 offer You my humble prayers
through the most Sacred Heart of Jesus,
Your most beloved Son,
our Lord and Redeemer,
in Whom You are always well pleased
and Who loves You so much.

In Your goodness,
grant me the grace of a lively faith,
a firm hope,
and an ardent love for You

and for my neighbor.
Grant me also the grace
to be truly sorry for all my sins
with a firm purpose of never offending You
again.
May I thus be able to live always
according to Your Divine good-pleasure,
to do Your most holy Will in all things
with a generous and willing heart,
and to persevere in Your love to the end of my
life.

Prayer to the Father for Spiritual Growth

Holy Lord,
Father Almighty,
Eternal God,
for the sake of Your generosity
and that of Your Son
Who endured suffering and death for me,
and for the sake of the wonderful holiness of
His Mother
and the merits of all the Saints,
grant to me,
a sinner unworthy of Your blessings,
that I may love You alone
and ever thirst for Your love.
Let me ever have in my heart
the remembrance of the benefits of the Passion.
May I recognize my own sinfulness
and desire to be humbled and deprecated by
all.
Let nothing grieve me except sin. St. Bonaventure

Prayer to the Father for the Benefits of Christ's Redemption

Eternal Father,
I offer You the infinite satisfaction
that Jesus rendered to Your justice
in behalf of sinners
on the tree of the Cross.
I ask that You would make available
the merits of His Precious Blood
to all guilty souls
to whom sin has brought death.
May they rise again to the life of grace
and glorify You forever.

Eternal Father,
I offer You the fervent devotion
of the Sacred Heart of Jesus
in satisfaction for the lukewarmness and cowardice
of Your chosen people.
By the burning love that made Him suffer death,
may You be pleased to rekindle their hearts,
which are now so lukewarm in Your service,
and to set them on fire with Your love
that they may love You forever.

Eternal Father,
I offer You
the submission of Jesus to Your Will.
Through His merits
may I receive the fullness of all grace
and accomplish Your Will entirely.
Blessed be God!   St. Margaret Mary Alacoque

Prayer of Thanksgiving to the Father

God and Father of our Lord Jesus Christ,
I thank You
because in Christ Your Son
You have blessed us
with every manner of spiritual blessing
in the heavenly realm.
These blessings correspond
to Your choice of us in Christ
before the foundation of the world,
that we should be holy and without blemish
in Your sight.

You have filled us
with the grace of Your Son
by imparting to us
all manner of wisdom and practical knowledge,
making known to us—
in keeping with Your good pleasure—
the Mystery of Your Will.
For this I thank You.

Prayer of Thanks
for the Father's Revelation in Christ

Eternal Father,
You are a Mystery for us
that if left to ourselves
we would never have discovered.
Your living Word,
Your Son, Jesus of Nazareth,

came among us
to reveal the way that leads to You.

O Father,
may You be thanked and praised for this way,
which is discovered by all
who come together in Jesus' Name
to pray to You with one heart.
For in that case
You listen to them
as if Your Son Himself were asking You
to listen to us and respond.
Praise to You for this great assurance
that You have granted us.

Prayer of Thanks for the Father's Love

Eternal Father,
we thank You for Your great love.
You give the world the best of Yourself,
the mirror of Your perfect transparency,
the splendor of Your very being—
Your Son Jesus.

We thank You for giving Him to us
not as a judge but as a Savior;
not as a tyrant but as a friend,
not as a commander but as a relative,
not as a superior but as a brother.

Help us to open our hearts
to His light
without fear of being overwhelmed
but exultant with the joy that comes from this
      light
upon all who accept it with gladness.

Prayer for Liberty and Life

Eternal Father,
I give You thanks
for setting me free from the law
of sin and death
by giving me the Spirit of life,
in Christ Jesus.
By sending Your Son as an offering
in the likeness of sinful flesh,
You have empowered me
to live not according to the flesh
but according to the Spirit.

You have thereby made it possible
for me to attain eternal life,
for Your Spirit dwells in me.
The Spirit Himself gives witness
with my spirit
that I am Your child.
And I am also an heir with Christ,
if only I suffer with Him
so as to be glorified with Him.

Prayer to the Father for Reconciliation

Heavenly Father,
in the Death and Resurrection
of Jesus Christ Your Son
You willed to reconcile all mankind
to Yourself
and so to reconcile all human beings
with each other in peace.
Hear the prayer of Your people.

Let Your Spirit of life and holiness renew us
in the depths of our being
and unite us throughout our life
to the risen Christ:
for He is our Brother and Savior.

With all Christians
we seek to follow the way of the Gospel.
Keep us faithful to the teachings of the Church
and alive to the needs of our neighbors.
Give us strength to work
for reconciliation, unity, and peace.
May those who seek the God they do not yet
    know
discover in You the source of light and hope.
May those who work for others
find strength in You.
May those who already know You
seek even further
and experience the depths of Your love.

Forgive us our sins,
deepen our faith,
kindle our hope,
and enliven our hearts with love.
May we walk in the footsteps of Jesus
as Your beloved sons and daughters.
With the help of Mary, our Mother,
may Your Church be the sign and sacrament
of salvation for all people,
that the world may believe in
Your love and Your truth.

Prayer to the Father,
Our Creator and Liberator

Father,
You are a living Person.
You are not an impersonal Owner
but a Father,
and Your glory is a person who is fully human.

You created us and gave us creativity;
You are responsible for our being here,
and You endowed us with responsibility.
You are eternally new
and You inspire us to seek ever new fulfillment
in accord with Your Divine Plan.

You are the liberating God of the Exodus
Who inspire us to seek true freedom con-
    stantly.
You help us to free ourselves from all selfish-
    ness
and to go out of ourselves to others
and to You.

You are infinite Love
and You invite us to be new persons
and bring Your love to others.
Grant us the power to labor in the world
with true freedom,
with honest creativity,
with ungrudging responsibility,
with complete selflessness,
and with unfeigned love for all.

Novena Prayer to God the Father

Heavenly Father, I adore You,
and I count myself as nothing
before Your Divine Majesty.
You alone are Being, Life, Truth, and Goodness.
Helpless and unworthy as I am,
I honor You, I praise You, I thank You,
and I love You in union with Jesus Christ,
Your Son, our Savior and our Brother,
in the merciful kindness of His Heart
and through His infinite merits.

I desire to serve You, to please You,
to obey You, and to love You always
in union with Mary Immaculate,
Mother of God and our Mother.
I also desire to love and serve my neighbor
for the love of You.

Heavenly Father,
thank You for making me Your child in Baptism.
With childlike confidence I ask You for this special favor: *(Mention Your request).*

I ask that Your Will may be done.
Give me what You know to be best for my soul,
and for the souls of those for whom I pray.
Give me Your Holy Spirit
to enlighten me and to guide me
in the way of Your commandments and holiness,
while I strive for the happiness of heaven
where I hope to glorify You forever.

Prayer in the Name of the Whole Christian People

We beg You, Master,
be our help and strength.
Save those among us who are oppressed,
have pity on the lowly, and lift up the fallen.
Heal the sick, bring back the straying,
and feed the hungry.
Release those in prison, steady those who falter,
and strengthen the fainthearted.
Let all nations come to know You the one God,
with Your Son Jesus Christ,
and us Your people and the sheep of Your pasture.

Do not keep count of the sins of Your servants
but purify us through the bath of Your truth
and direct our steps.
Help us to walk in holiness of heart,
and to do what is good and pleasing in Your
eyes
and in the eyes of our rulers.

Master, let Your face shine on us
to grant us every good in peace,
to protect us by Your powerful hand,
to deliver us from every evil by the might of
Your arm,
and to save us from the unjust hatred of our
enemies.
Grant to us and all who dwell on this earth
peace and harmony, O Lord.

St. Clement I

GOD THE SON —OUR REDEEMER AND BROTHER

Our knowledge of God is communicated to us primarily by God the Son made Man, Jesus Christ. In Him we have access to the Father. By entrusting ourselves to Him in prayer we attain our true goal in life.

Jesus Christ is the center of the Father's work of salvation because He is the Son of God made Man so that as perfect Man He might save all people and sum up all things in Himself. He summed up in Himself the Mysteries of our salvation by His Death and His Resurrection; He had received all power in heaven and on earth; He founded His Church as a means for our salvation. Hence, in Christ our Redeemer we are joined to all human beings.

By becoming Man, Jesus consecrated human experience; God, now one of us, can be found in human loving, striving, and hoping. The risen Jesus is the firstfruits that includes the entire harvest of mankind, having died to a world where sin is at home and risen to the full humanity of the new creation.

Jesus poured out on His people the Spirit of adoption by making us children of God. He made for Himself a new people, filled with the grace of God. United with Jesus, this new People of God constitutes "the whole Christ." He offers them to His Father and gives Him glory. This is the aim of His Father's plan for the salvation of all people.

As we know, many of our prayers are directed to the Father through Jesus in the Holy Spirit. However, we also should pray directly to Jesus since He is the image of the unseen God (Colossians 1:15). As we pray, we can form a picture of Him in our minds—something that we cannot easily do concerning God the Father.

(We might point out that, besides the special prayers found in this section, we can also make

*use of any of the prayers to Jesus the Redeemer
in the section "Official Prayers of the Church," pp.
24-30.)*

PRAYERS TO JESUS,
TRUE GOD AND TRUE MAN

Litany to God the Son

O Jesus, Who for love of me consented to be-
    come Man,
I thank You with all my heart.
O Jesus, Who for love of me
passed nine months in the womb of a Virgin, *
O Jesus, Who for love of me
willed to be born in a poor stable, *
O Jesus, Who for love of me
worked in the sweat of Your brow, *
O Jesus, Who for love of me
suffered a painful Passion, *
O Jesus, Who for love of me
hung on the Cross for three hours
and died in ignominy on it, *
O Jesus, Who from the Cross gave me Mary to
    be my Mother, *
O Jesus, Who ascended to heaven, to prepare a
    place for me
and to make Yourself my Advocate with the
    Father, *
O Jesus, Who for love of me
reside day and night in the tabernacle, *
O Jesus, Who for love of me

immolate Yourself every morning on the altar,*
O Jesus, Who come so often into my heart
by Holy Communion,*
O Jesus, Who in the holy tribunal
so often wash me in Your precious Blood,*

Prayer to Jesus, True Man

O Jesus,
You are true Man.
You took upon Yourself a human body and
    soul,
You thought with a human mind,
and You acted through a human Will.

But You are far above every other human.
No one ever spoke like You,
with such authority, freedom, and gentleness,
indicating the paths of love, justice, and sincer-
    ity,
and no one ever matched Your teachings.
You spoke about the Mystery of God
in a way so elevated above others
that You make it possible for us
to have a sublime experience of God,
to come to know Him
and achieve a living love for Him.

O Jesus,
no one ever acted like You, either.
You left us an example of the perfect human
    life:
by Your preference for poverty,
by Your love for the poor and the sick,

by Your concern for the suffering,
by Your liberating message of salvation,
by Your espousal of peace and service,
by Your obedience to the Father—
even to the death of the Cross.

O Jesus,
help us to know You more
so that we may know ourselves more.
Help us to live with You
so that we may live fully human lives.
Satisfy our human hunger with Yourself,
Who are the Man for others and for God,
the Man with others and with God,
perfect Love,
the Man-Who-is-Love,
and the God-Who-is-Love.

Prayer to Jesus, True God

O Jesus,
You are the Son of God.
Hence, not only do You resolve our problems
and respond to our aspirations.
You also do so with unexpected fullness.

As the Son sent to us by the Father,
You are the God Who comes to meet us
and manifests for us
the God Whom we seek in groping fashion.

You are the revelation of God for us—
the full, perfect, and definitive revelation—
God in person.

In You
the God-Who-is-far-off
becomes the God-Who-is-near,
the God-with-us,
and the God-Who-is-one-of-us,
our companion on life's journey.
You alone, O Lord,
are the Way, the Truth, and the Life,
the Messiah,
and the Son of the living God.

Invocations to Christ

We adore You,
the Most Holy One.
You abased Yourself and have lifted us up.
You humbled Yourself and have honored us.
You became poor and have enriched us.

You were born and have given us life.
You received baptism and have cleansed us.
You fasted and have filled us.
You fought and have given us strength.

You sat on a donkey
and have taken us into Your cortege.
You appeared before the tribunal
and have offered us.
You were led as a prisoner before the high
    priest
and have set us free.
You were subjected to questioning
and have let us sit as judges.
You kept silence

and have instructed us.
You were whipped like a slave
and have given us freedom.
You were deprived of Your clothing
and have clothed us.

You were tied to a column
and have loosed our bonds.
You were crucified
and have saved us.
You tasted the vinegar
and have given us delightful drink.
You were crowned with thorns
and have made us kings.

You died and have made us live.
You were placed in a tomb and have revived us.
You rose in glory and have given us joy.
You clothed Yourself in glory
and have filled us with admiration.
You ascended to heaven and have taken us
with You.
You are seated in glory and have elevated us.
You sent us the Holy Spirit and have sanctified
us.

Blessed be You Who come
all radiant with goodness!   Maronite Rite

Prayer To "Learn" Christ

T each me,
Lord,
to be mild and gentle in all the events of life—
in disappointments,

in the thoughtlessness of others,
in the insincerity of those I trusted,
in the unfaithfulness of those on whom I relied.

Let me put myself aside,
to think of the happiness of others,
to hide my little pains and heartaches,
so that I may be the only one to suffer from
them.

Teach me to profit by the suffering
that comes across my path.
Let me so use it that it may mellow me,
not harden or embitter me;
that it may make me patient, not irritable;
that it may make me broad in my forgiveness,
not narrow, haughty, and overbearing.

May no one be less good
for having come within my influence;
no one less pure, less true, less kind, less noble
for having been a fellow-pilgrim
on our journey toward eternal life.

As I go my rounds from one distraction to another,
let me whisper from time to time a word of
love to You.
May my life be lived in the supernatural,
full of power for good,
and strong in its purpose of sanctity.

Petitions to Jesus

O good Jesus:
Word of the eternal Father, convert me.

Son of Mary, take me as her child.
My Master, teach me.
Prince of peace, give me peace.
My Refuge, receive me.
My Shepherd, feed my soul.
Model of patience, comfort me.

Meek and humble of Heart, help me to become
    like You.
My Redeemer, save me.
My God and my All, possess me.
The true Way, direct me.
Eternal Truth, instruct me.
Life of the Saints, make me live in You.
My Support, strengthen me.
My Justice, justify me.
My Mediator with the Father, reconcile me.
Physician of my soul, heal me.
My Judge, pardon me.
My King, rule me.

My Sanctification, sanctify me.
Abyss of goodness, pardon me.
Living Bread from heaven, nourish me.
Father of the prodigal, receive me.
Joy of my soul, be my only happiness.
My Helper, assist me.
Magnet of love, draw me.
My Protector, defend me.
My Hope, sustain me.
Object of my love, unite me to Yourself.
Fountain of life, refresh me.
My Divine Victim, atone for me.

My Last End, let me possess You.
My Glory, glorify me.

Novena Prayer to Jesus

Jesus,
I believe that by Your own power
You rose from death as You promised,
a glorious Victor.
May this Mystery strengthen my hope
in another and better life after death,
the resurrection of my body on the last day,
and an eternity of happiness.

I firmly hope that You will keep Your promise
　　to me
and raise me up glorified.
Through Your glorious Resurrection
I hope that You will make my body
like Your own in glory and life,
and permit me to dwell with You
in heaven for all eternity.

I believe that Your Resurrection is the crown
of Your life and work as God-Man,
because it is Your glorification.
This is the beginning of the glorious life
that was due to You as the Son of God.

Your Resurrection is also the reward
of Your life and suffering.
Jesus, my Risen Lord and King,
I adore Your Sacred Humanity,
which receives this eternal Kingdom
of honor, power, joy, and glory.

I rejoice with You, my Master,
glorious, immortal, and all-powerful.

Through the glorious Mystery
of Your Resurrection,
I ask You to help me rise with You spiritually
and to live a life free from sin,
so that I may be bent upon doing God's Will
in all things,
and may be patient in suffering.
Through the Sacraments
may my soul be enriched evermore
with sanctifying grace,
the source of Divine Life.
I also ask that You grant me
this special request: *(Mention your request).*
May Your Will be done.

DAILY PRAYERS

Morning Offering

O Jesus,
through the Immaculate Heart of Mary,
I offer You my prayers, works, joys, and sufferings
of this day
in union with the Holy Sacrifice of the Mass
throughout the world.
I offer them
for all the intentions of Your Sacred Heart:
the salvation of souls,
reparation for sins,
the reunion of all Christians.

I offer them for the intentions of our Bishops
and of all the Apostles of Prayer,
and in particular for those
recommended by our Holy Father for this
     month. Apostleship of Prayer

Prayer for God's Protection
and Christ's Presence

As I arise today,
may the strength of God pilot me,
the power of God uphold me,
the wisdom of God guide me.

May the eye of God look before me,
the ear of God hear me,
the word of God speak for me.

May the hand of God protect me,
the way of God lie before me,
the shield of God defend me,
the host of God save me.

May Christ shield me today . . .
Christ with me, Christ before me,
Christ behind me,
Christ in me, Christ beneath me,
Christ above me,

Christ on my right, Christ on my left,
Christ when I lie down, Christ when I sit,
Christ when I stand,

Christ in the heart of everyone
who thinks of me,

Christ in the mouth of everyone
who speaks of me,

Christ in every eye that sees me,
Christ in every ear that hears me.   St. Patrick

Midafternoon Prayer

O Divine Savior,
I transport myself in spirit to Mount Calvary
to ask pardon for my sins,
for it was because of humankind's sins
that You chose to offer Yourself in sacrifice.
I thank You for Your extraordinary generosity
and I am also grateful to You
for making me a child of Mary, Your Mother.

Blessed Mother, take me under your protec-
tion.
St. John, you took Mary under your care.
Teach me true devotion to Mary, the Mother of
God.
May the Father, the Son, and the Holy Spirit
be glorified in all places
through the Immaculate Virgin Mary.

Evening Prayer

I adore You, my God,
and thank You for having created me,
for having made me a Christian,
and for having preserved me this day.
I love You with all my heart
and I am sorry for having sinned against You,

because You are infinite Love and infinite
    Goodness.
Protect me during my rest
and may Your love be always with me.

Eternal Father,
I offer You the precious Blood of Jesus Christ
in atonement for my sins
and for all the intentions of our holy Church.

Holy Spirit, Love of the Father and the Son,
purify my heart and fill it with the fire of Your
    Love,
so that I may be a chaste Temple of the Holy
    Trinity
and be always pleasing to You in all things.

Petitions of St. Augustine

Lord Jesus, let me know myself; let me know
    You,
And desire nothing else but You.
Let me hate myself and love You,
And do all things for the sake of You.
Let me humble myself and exalt You,
And think of nothing else but You.
Let me die to myself and live in You,
And take whatever happens as coming from
    You.
Let me forsake myself and walk after You,
And ever desire to follow You.
Let me flee from myself and turn to You,
That so I may merit to be defended by You.

Let me fear for myself, let me fear You,
And be among those that are chosen by You.
Let me distrust myself and trust in You,
And ever obey for the love of You.
Let me cleave to nothing but You,
And ever be poor because of You.
Look upon me that I may love You,
Call me, that I may see You,
And forever possess You, for all eternity.

Night Prayer

Jesus Christ, my God,
I adore You
and I thank You for the many favors
You have bestowed on me this day.
I offer You my sleep
and all the moments of this night,
and I pray You to preserve me from sin.
Therefore, I place myself
in Your most sacred Side
and under the mantle of our Blessed Lady,
my Mother.
May the holy Angels assist me
and keep me in peace,
and may Your blessing be upon me

Prayer for the Faithful Departed

O Lord Jesus Christ, King of glory,
deliver the souls of all the faithful departed
from the pains of hell
and from the bottomless pit.

Deliver them from the lion's mouth,
that hell swallow them not up,
that they fall not into darkness,
but let the holy standard-bearer Michael
bring them into that holy light which You
    promised
to Abraham and his seed.

CONFESSION PRAYERS

Prayer before Confession

Receive my confession,
O most loving and gracious Lord Jesus Christ,
only hope for the salvation of my soul.
Grant to me true contrition of soul,
so that day and night I may by penance
make satisfaction for my many sins.
Savior of the world, O good Jesus,
Who gave Yourself to the death on the Cross
to save sinners,
look upon me, most wretched of all sinners,
have pity on me,
and give me the light to know my sins,
true sorrow for them,
and a purpose of never committing them
    again.

O gracious Virgin Mary,
Immaculate Mother of Jesus,
I implore you to obtain for me
by your powerful intercession
these graces from your Divine Son.

St. Joseph, pray for me.

Prayer after Confession

My dearest Jesus,
I have told all my sins as well as I could.
I have tried hard to make a good confession.
I feel sure that You have forgiven me.
I thank You.
It is only because of all Your sufferings
that I can go to confession
and free myself from my sins.
Your Heart is full of love and mercy
for poor sinners.
I love You because You are so good to me.

My loving Savior,
I shall try to keep from sin
and to love You more each day.
My dear Mother Mary,
pray for me and help me to keep my promises.
Protect me and do not let me fall back into
    sin.

PRAYERS BEFORE HOLY COMMUNION

Act of Faith

Lord Jesus Christ,
I firmly believe that You are present
in this Blessed Sacrament
as true God and true Man,
with Your Body and Blood,
Soul and Divinity.
My Redeemer and my Judge,

I adore Your Divine Majesty
in union with the Angels and Saints.
I believe, O Lord;
increase my faith.

Act of Hope

Good Jesus,
in You alone I place all my hope.
You are my salvation and my strength,
the source of all good.
Through Your mercy,
through Your Passion and Death,
I hope to obtain the pardon of my sins,
the grace of final perseverance,
and a happy eternity.

Act of Love

Jesus, my God,
I love You with my whole heart
and above all things,
because You are the one supreme Good
and an infinitely perfect Being.
You have given Your life for me, a poor sinner,
and in Your mercy
You have even offered Yourself
as food for my soul.

My God,
I love You.
Inflame my heart
so that I may love You more.

Act of Contrition

O my Savior,
I am truly sorry for having offended You
because You are infinitely good
and sin displeases You.
I detest all the sins of my life
and I desire to atone for them.
Through the merits of Your precious Blood,
wash me of all stain of sin,
so that entirely cleansed
I may worthily approach
the most holy Sacrament of the altar.

My heart yearns to receive You
in Holy Communion.
Come, Bread of Heaven and Food of Angels,
to nourish my soul
and rejoice my heart.
Come, most lovable Friend of my soul,
to inflame me with such love
that I may never again be separated from You.

PRAYERS AFTER
HOLY COMMUNION

Act of Faith

J esus,
I firmly believe that You are present within me
as God and Man,
to enrich my soul with graces
and to fill my heart

with the happiness of the blessed
I believe that You are Christ,
the Son of the living God.

Act of Adoration

With deepest humility,
I adore You,
my Lord and my God;
You have made my soul Your dwelling place.
I adore You as my Creator
from Whose hands I came
and with Whom I am to be happy forever.

Act of Love

Dear Jesus,
I love You with my whole heart,
with my whole soul,
and with all my strength.
May the love of Your own Sacred Heart
fill my soul and purify it
so that I may die to the world for love of You,
as You died on the Cross for love of me.
My God,
You are all mine;
grant that I may be all Yours
in time and in eternity.

Act of Thanksgiving

Dear Lord,
I thank You from the depths of my heart

for Your infinite kindness in coming to me.
With Your most holy Mother
and all the Angels,
I praise Your mercy and generosity
toward me, a poor sinner.
I thank You for nourishing my soul
with Your Sacred Body and Precious Blood.
I will try to show my gratitude to You
in the Sacrament of Your love,
by obedience to Your holy commandments,
by fidelity to my duties,
by kindness to my neighbor,
and by an earnest endeavor
to become more like You
in my daily conduct

Prayer to Our Redeemer

Soul of Christ, sanctify me.
Body of Christ, save me.
Blood of Christ, inebriate me.
Water from the side of Christ, wash me.
Passion of Christ, strengthen me.
O good Jesus, hear me.
Within Your wounds, hide me.
Separated from You let me never be.
From the malignant enemy, defend me.
At the hour of death, call me.
To come to You, bid me,
That I may praise You in the company
Of Your Saints, for all eternity.

Prayer To See Jesus in Others

Through this Holy Communion,
I beg You, O Lord Jesus,
for the grace ever to love You
in my neighbor.
Let me see in every human being
Your own dear self—disguised but really there.
Since every human being is a potential member
of Your Mystical Body,
I want to make my every act
a personal service rendered to You.

Your new law demands that I avoid
not only bodily injury to my neighbor
but also angry and uncharitable words and
    emotions.
Let me never put limits to my forgiveness,
so that Your Father may forgive me my of-
    fenses.
Through this Communion
make me a living example
of Your great commandment of love.

Look Down Upon Me,
Good and Gentle Jesus

Look down upon me,
good and gentle Jesus,
while before Your face I humbly kneel,
and with burning soul pray and beseech You
to fix deep in my heart
lively sentiments of faith, hope and charity,

true contrition for my sins,
and a firm purpose of amendment,
while I contemplate with great love and tender
    pity
Your five wounds,
pondering over them within me,
calling to mind the words that David, Your
    Prophet,
said of You, my good Jesus:
"They have pierced My hands and My feet;
they have numbered all My bones" (Psalm
    22:17-18).

PRAYERS TO JESUS IN THE BLESSED SACRAMENT

Prayer of Adoration and Petition

I adore You,
O Jesus,
true God and true Man,
here present in the Holy Eucharist,
as I humbly kneel before You
and unite myself in spirit
with all the faithful on earth
and all the Saints in heaven.
In heartfelt gratitude for so great a blessing,
I love You,
my Jesus,
with my whole soul,
for You are infinitely perfect
and all worthy of my love.

Give me the grace
nevermore in any way to offend You.
Grant that I may be renewed
by Your Eucharistic presence here on earth
and be found worthy to arrive with Mary
at the enjoyment
of Your eternal and blessed presence in heaven.

Prayer of Reparation

With the deep and humble feeling
that the Faith inspires in me,
O my God and Savior, Jesus Christ,
true God and true Man,
I love You with all my heart,
and I adore You Who are hidden here.
I do so in reparation
for all the irreverences, profanations, and sac-
    rileges
that You receive
in the most august Sacrament of the altar.

I adore You, O my God,
not so much as You are worthy to be adored,
nor so much as I am bound to do,
but at least as much as I am able.
Would that I could adore You
with the perfect worship
that the Angels in heaven are able to offer You.

O Jesus,
may You be known, adored, loved, and thanked
by all people at every moment
in this most holy and Divine Sacrament.

Act of Spiritual Communion

My Jesus,
I believe that You are in the Blessed Sacra-
ment.
I love You above all things,
and I long for You in my soul.
Since I cannot now receive You sacramentally,
come at least spiritually into my heart.
As though You have already come,
I embrace You and unite myself entirely to
You;
never permit me to be separated from You.

O Sacred Banquet

O sacred banquet,
in which Christ is received,
the memory of His Passion is renewed,
the mind is filled with grace,
and a pledge of future glory is given to us.

℣. You have given them bread from heaven.
℟. *Containing in itself all sweetness.*

Let us pray.
O God,
You have left us a remembrance of Your Passion
beneath the veils of this Sacrament.
Grant us, we pray,
so to venerate the sacred Mysteries
of Your Body and Blood
that we may always enjoy the fruits

of Your Redemption.
You live and reign forever.

Hidden God, Devoutly I Adore You

Hidden God, devoutly I adore You,
Truly present underneath these veils:
All my heart subdues itself before You
Since it all before You faints and fails.

Not to sight, or taste, or touch be credit,
Hearing only do we trust secure;
I believe, for God the Son has said it—
Word of Truth that ever shall endure.

On the Cross was veiled Your Godhead's splen-
    dor,
Here Your manhood lies hidden too;
Unto both alike my faith I render,
And, as sued the contrite thief, I sue.

Though I look not on Your wounds with
    Thomas,
You, my Lord, and You, my God, I call:
Make me more and more believe Your promise,
Hope in You, and love You over all.

O memorial of my Savior dying,
Living Bread, that gives life to man;
Make my soul, its life from You supplying,
Taste Your sweetness, as on earth it can.

Deign, O Jesus, Pelican of heaven,
Me, a sinner, in Your Blood to lave,
To a single drop of which is given
All the world from all its sin to save.

Contemplating, Lord, Your hidden presence,
Grant me what I thirst for and implore,
In the revelation of Your essence
To behold Your glory evermore.

PRAYERS TO THE
SACRED HEART OF JESUS

Prayer of Consecration

I, N . . . , give myself
to the Sacred Heart of our Lord Jesus Christ,
and I consecrate to Him
my person and my life,
my actions, pains, and sufferings,
so that henceforth I shall be unwilling
to make use of any part of my being
except for the honor, love, and glory
of the Sacred Heart.

My unchanging purpose is to be all His
and to do all things for the love of Him
while renouncing with all my heart
whatever is displeasing to Him.

I take You,
O Sacred Heart,
as the only object of my love,
the guardian of my life,
the assurance of my salvation,
the remedy of my weakness and inconstancy,
the atonement for all my faults,
and the sure refuge at my death.

O Heart of goodness,
be my justification before God the Father,
and turn away from me
the strokes of His righteous anger.

O Heart of love,
I place all my trust in You,
for I fear everything
from my own wickedness and frailty,
but I hope for all things
from Your goodness and bounty.

Consume in me all that can displease You
or resist Your holy Will.
Let Your pure love imprint You
so deeply upon my heart
that I shall nevermore be able to forget You
or be separated from You.
May I obtain from all Your loving kindness
the grace of having my name written in You,
for I desire to place in You
all my happiness and all my glory,
living and dying in virtual bondage to You.

St. Margaret Mary Alacoque

Prayer for Enlightenment

Sacred Heart of Jesus,
teach me an entire forgetfulness of myself,
since there is no other way of reaching You.
Grant that I may do nothing that is unworthy
     of You.

Teach me what I ought to do
to attain to Your pure love,

for You have inspired me with this desire.
I feel in myself a great longing to please You.
But I am helpless
without Your special light and strength.

O Lord,
do Your Will in me,
though I often opposed it in the past.
You must do all,
Divine Heart of Jesus.
It shall be Your glory alone if I become a Saint,
and it is for Your glory alone
that I desire to be perfect.   St. Claude de la Colombiere

Litany of the
Most Sacred Heart of Jesus

Lord, have mercy.
Christ, have mercy.
Lord, have mercy.
Christ, hear us.
Christ, graciously hear us.
God the Father of heaven,
  have mercy on us.
God the Son, Redeemer of
  the world,*
God, the Holy Spirit,
Holy Trinity, one God,
Heart of Jesus, Son of the
  Eternal Father,
Heart of Jesus, formed by
  the Holy Spirit in the
  womb   of   the   Virgin
  Mother,
Heart of Jesus, substantially
united to the Word of
  God,
Heart of Jesus, of infinite
  majesty,
Heart of Jesus, sacred tem-
  ple of God,
Heart of Jesus, tabernacle
  of the Most High,
Heart of Jesus, house of
  God and gate of heaven,
Heart of Jesus, burning fur-
  nace of charity,
Heart of Jesus, abode of jus-
  tice and love,
Heart of Jesus, full of good-
  ness and love,
Heart of Jesus, abyss of all
  virtues,

* *Have mercy on us* is repeated after each invocation.

Heart of Jesus, most worthy of all praise,

Heart of Jesus, king and center of all hearts,

Heart of Jesus, in Whom are all the treasures of wisdom and knowledge,

Heart of Jesus, in Whom dwells the fullness of Divinity,

Heart of Jesus, in Whom the Father was well pleased,

Heart of Jesus, of Whose fullness we have all received,

Heart of Jesus, desire of the everlasting hills,

Heart of Jesus, patient and most merciful,

Heart of Jesus, enriching all who invoke You,

Heart of Jesus, fountain of life and holiness,

Heart of Jesus, propitiation for our sins,

Heart of Jesus, loaded down with opprobrium,

Heart of Jesus, bruised for our offenses,

Heart of Jesus, obedient to death,

Heart of Jesus, pierced with a lance,

Heart of Jesus, source of all consolation,

Heart of Jesus, our life and resurrection,

Heart of Jesus, our peace and reconciliation,

Heart of Jesus, victim for our sins,

Heart of Jesus, salvation of those who trust in You,

Heart of Jesus, hope of those who die in You,

Heart of Jesus, delight of all the Saints,

Lamb of God, You take away the sins of the world; *spare us, O Lord*

Lamb of God, You take away the sins of the world; *graciously hear us, O Lord*

Lamb of God, You take away the sins of the world; *have mercy on us.*

℣. Jesus, meek and humble of Heart.

℟. *Make our hearts like to Yours.*

Let us pray.

Almighty and Eternal God,
look upon the Heart of Your most beloved Son
and upon the praises and satisfaction
that He offers You in the name of sinners;

and to those who implore Your mercy,
in Your great goodness, grant forgiveness
in the Name of the same Jesus Christ, Your
    Son,
Who lives and reigns with You, forever and
    ever.

Prayer To Receive Continuous Help

O loving Heart of our Lord Jesus Christ,
You move hearts that are harder than rock,
You melt spirits that are colder than ice,
and You reach souls that are more impenetra-
    ble than diamonds.
Touch my heart with Your sacred wounds
and permeate my soul with Your Precious
    Blood,
so that wherever I turn
I will see only my Divine Crucified Lord,
and everything I see
will appear colored with Your Blood.

Lord Jesus,
let my heart never rest until it finds You,
Who are its center, its love, and its happi-
    ness.
By the wound in Your Heart,
pardon the sins that I have committed
whether out of malice or out of evil desires.
Place my weak heart in Your own Divine
    Heart,

continually under Your protection and guidance,
so that I may persevere in doing good
and in fleeing evil until my last breath.

Heart of Jesus, save me.
Heart of my Creator, perfect me.
Heart of my Savior, deliver me.
Heart of my Judge, forgive me.
Heart of my Father, govern me.
Heart of my Spouse, love me.
Heart of my Master, teach me.

Heart of my King, crown me.
Heart of my Benefactor, enrich me.
Heart of my Pastor, defend me.
Heart of my Friend, embrace me.
Heart of my Infant Jesus, draw me.
Heart of Jesus dying on the Cross,
    pray for me.
Heart of Jesus, I greet You in all Your states.
Give Yourself to me.

St. Margaret Mary Alacoque

PRAYERS TO CHRIST THE KING

Act of Dedication of the Human Race to Jesus Christ, King

Most sweet Jesus,
Redeemer of the human race,
look down upon us humbly prostrate before
    You.

We are Yours, and Yours we wish to be;
but to be more surely united with You,
behold, each one of us freely consecrates himself today
to Your Most Sacred Heart.
Many indeed have never known You;
many, too, despising Your precepts,
have rejected You.
Have mercy on them all, most merciful Jesus,
and draw them to Your Sacred Heart.

Be King, O Lord,
not only of the faithful who have never for-
saken You,
but also of the prodigal children who have
abandoned You;
grant that they may quickly return to their
Father's house,
lest they die of wretchedness and hunger.

Be King of those who are deceived by erroneous opinions,
or whom discord keeps aloof,
and call them back to the harbor of truth
and the unity of faith,
so that soon there may be but one flock and
one Shepherd.

Grant, O Lord, to Your Church
assurance of freedom and immunity from
harm;
give tranquillity of order to all nations;
make the earth resound from pole to pole with
one cry:

Praise to the Divine Heart that wrought our
    salvation;
to It be glory and honor for ever.

Consecration

O Christ Jesus,
I acknowledge You as King of the Universe.
All that has been made has been created for
    You.
Make full use of Your rights over me.
I renew the promises I made in Baptism,
when I renounced Satan
and all his pomps and works.
I promise to live a good Christian life.
Especially, I undertake to help,
to the extent of my means,
to secure the triumph of the rights of God
and of Your Church.

Divine Heart of Jesus,
I offer You my poor efforts
so that all hearts may acknowledge
Your sacred Royalty,
and the Kingdom of Your peace may be estab-
    lished
throughout the entire universe.

GOD THE HOLY SPIRIT—
OUR SANCTIFIER AND GUIDE

The Holy Spirit guides us in the way of sanctification and salvation. As He descended on Jesus at His Baptism by John, so He descends on us at Baptism and inspires us to a loving union with God through actions and prayer.

PRAYERS TO GOD THE HOLY SPIRIT

The Holy Spirit is the Third Person of the Blessed Trinity, really God just as the Father and the Son are really God. He is the Love of the Father and the Son. As Jesus is the center of the History of Salvation so the Mystery of God is the center from which this History takes its origin and to which it is ordered as to its last end. The risen Jesus leads human beings to the Father by sending the Holy Spirit upon the People of God.

By His new and deeper coming into the world at Pentecost, the Spirit was to accomplish the salvation of humanity. He came to sanctify the Church forever, giving life to all people because He is the Spirit of life. He is the very soul of the Church.

The Spirit prays and bears witness in the faithful that they are adopted children of God. He guides the Church into the fullness of truth and gives her a unity of fellowship and service, furnishes and directs her with various gifts, and adorns her with the fruits of His grace. By the power of the Gospel He makes the Church grow, renews her constantly, and leads her to perfect unity with her Spouse, Jesus Christ.

Every Christian receives the Holy Spirit in Baptism and Confirmation. Through Him we share in the life of grace, God's life in our souls. By His presence we are continually moved to have communion with God and our fellow human beings and to fulfill our duties.

The Spirit has always been something of a "forgotten" Person. The prayers found in this section are intended to enable all Catholics to love and

*adore this wondrous Spirit Who dwells within us
constantly.*

*(We might point out that, besides the special
prayers found in this section, we can also make
use of any of the prayers to God the Holy Spirit in
the section "Official Prayers of the Church," pp.
30-36.)*

Prayer To Receive the Holy Spirit

O King of glory,
send us the Promised of the Father,
the Spirit of Truth.
May the Counselor Who proceeds from You
enlighten us
and infuse all truth in us,
as You have promised.

Prayer for the Seven Gifts of the Spirit

O Lord Jesus,
through You I humbly beg the merciful Father
to send the Holy Spirit of grace,
that He may bestow upon us His sevenfold
    gifts.

May He send us the gift of *wisdom*,
which will make us relish the Tree of Life
that is none other than Yourself;
the gift of *understanding*,
which will enlighten us;
the gift of *counsel*,
which will guide us in the way of righteous-
    ness;

and the gift of *fortitude,*
which will give us the strength to vanquish
the enemies of our sanctification and salvation.

May He impart to us the gift of *knowledge,*
which will enable us to discern Your teaching
and distinguish good from evil;
the gift of *piety,*
which will make us enjoy true peace;
and the gift of *fear,*
which will make us shun all iniquity
and avoid all danger of offending Your Majesty.

To the Father
and to the Son
and to the Holy Spirit
be given all glory and thanksgiving forever.

St. Bonaventure

Prayer for the Twelve Fruits of the Spirit

Holy Spirit,
eternal Love of the Father and the Son,
kindly bestow on us
the fruit of *charity,*
that we may be united to You by Divine love;
the fruit of *joy,*
that we may be filled with holy consolation;
the fruit of *peace,*
that we may enjoy tranquillity of soul;
and the fruit of *patience,*
that we may endure humbly
everything that may be opposed to our own desires.

Divine Spirit,
be pleased to infuse in us
the fruit of *benignity,*
that we may willingly relieve our neighbor's
    necessities;
the fruit of *goodness,*
that we may be benevolent toward all;
the fruit of *longanimity,*
that we may not be discouraged by delay
but may persevere in prayer;
and the fruit of *mildness,*
that we may subdue every rising of ill temper,
stifle every murmur,
and repress the susceptibilities of our nature
in all our dealings with our neighbor.

Creator Spirit,
graciously impart to us
the fruit of *fidelity,*
that we may rely with assured confidence
on the Word of God;
the fruit of *modesty,*
that we may order our exterior regularly;
and the fruits of *continence* and *chastity,*
that we may keep our bodies in such holiness
as befits Your temple,
so that having by Your assistance
preserved our hearts pure on earth,
we may merit in Jesus Christ,
according to the words of the Gospel,
to see God eternally
in the glory of His Kingdom.

Prayer for Union with the Holy Spirit

O Holy Spirit of Light and Love,
to You I consecrate my heart, mind, and will
for time and eternity.
May I be ever docile to Your Divine inspirations
and to the teachings of the holy Catholic
  Church
whose infallible guide You are.

May my heart be ever inflamed
with the love of God and love of neighbor.
May my will be ever in harmony with Your Divine Will.
May my life faithfully imitate the life and virtues
of our Lord and Savior Jesus Christ.
To Him,
with the Father,
and You, Divine Spirit,
be honor and glory forever.   St. Pius X

Prayer for the Indwelling of the Spirit

Holy Spirit,
powerful Consoler,
sacred Bond of the Father and the Son,
Hope of the afflicted,
descend into my heart
and establish in it Your loving dominion.
Enkindle in my tepid soul
the fire of Your Love
so that I may be wholly subject to You.

We believe that when You dwell in us,
You also prepare a dwelling

for the Father and the Son.
Deign, therefore, to come to me,
Consoler of abandoned souls
and Protector of the needy.
Help the afflicted,
strengthen the weak,
and support the wavering.

Come and purify me.
Let no evil desire take possession of me.
You love the humble and resist the proud.
Come to me,
glory of the living
and hope of the dying.
Lead me by Your grace
that I may always be pleasing to You.

St. Augustine of Hippo

Prayer to the Holy Spirit for Unbelievers

H oly Spirit,
on the first Pentecost,
through Your inspiration many were trans-
    formed,
becoming adopted children of God
and faithful disciples of Jesus Christ.
They were animated by the love of God
that is poured into us
by You, Holy Spirit,
Who are given to us.

Enlighten the minds of unbelievers,
incline their wills to accept the Good News,

and prompt them to be obedient
to the Teachers of the Church
about whom Christ said:
"He who hears you hears Me;
he who rejects you rejects Me" (Luke 10:16).
Teach them how to pray
and prepare their minds and hearts
for Your coming into their souls.

Prayer for the Propagation of the Faith

O Holy Spirit,
You desire the salvation of all human beings
and for that purpose You want all of them
to acquire the knowledge of Your Truth.
Grant to all of them
Your powerful Light and Your Love of Good-
    will
that they may give glory to God
in unity of faith, hope, and love.
Send laborers into the harvest
who are truly animated by You,
Who are the Soul of the missionary Church.

Prayer of Spouses to the Spirit

O Holy Spirit,
Spirit of unity,
Love and Goodwill of Father and Son,
You have made us one in the sacred union of
    marriage.
Grant that—like the first Christians—
we may be of one heart and one mind.

Make us respect one another,
help one another in our striving for holiness,
and support one another.
Be our Guide,
our Counselor,
and our Consoler.
Make us bear one another's burdens
during our journey to heaven
where we hope to live forever
as adopted children of the Triune God.

Litany of the Holy Spirit

(For Private Devotion)

Lord, have mercy.
Christ, have mercy.
Lord, have mercy.
Holy Spirit, hear us.
Holy Spirit, graciously hear us.
God, the Father of heaven, *have mercy on us*
God, the Son, Redeemer of the world,*
God, the Holy Spirit,
Holy Trinity, one God,
Holy Spirit, Who proceed from the Father,
Holy Spirit, coequal with the Father and the Son,
Promise of the Father, most bounteous,
Gift of God most high,
Ray of heavenly Light,
Author of all good,
Source of living Water,
Consuming Fire,
Burning Love,
Spiritual Unction,
Spirit of truth and power,
Spirit of wisdom and understanding,
Spirit of counsel and fortitude,
Spirit of knowledge and piety,
Spirit of fear of the Lord,
Spirit of compunction,
Spirit of grace and prayer,
Spirit of charity, peace, and joy,
Spirit of patience,
Spirit of longanimity and goodness,

Have mercy on us is repeated after each invocation.

Spirit of benignity and mildness,

Spirit of fidelity,

Spirit of modesty and continence,

Spirit of chastity,

Spirit of adoption of sons of God,

Holy Spirit, comforter,

Holy Spirit, sanctifier,

You through Whom spoke holy men of God,

You Who overshadowed Mary,

You by Whom Mary conceived Christ,

You Who descend upon men at Baptism,

You Who, on the Day of Pentecost, appeared through fiery tongues,

You by Whom we are reborn,

You Who dwell in us as in a temple,

You Who govern and animate the Church,

You Who fill the whole world,

That You may renew the face of the earth, *we beseech You, hear us.*

That You may shed Your Light upon us,**

That You may pour Your Love into our hearts,

That You may inspire us to love our neighbor,

That You may teach us to ask for the graces we need,

That You may enlighten us with Your heavenly inspirations,

That You may guide us in the way of holiness,

That You may make us obedient to Your Commandments,

That You may teach us how to pray,

That You may always pray with us,

That You may inspire us with horror for sin,

That You may direct us in the practice of virtue,

That You may make us persevere in a holy life.

That You may make us faithful to our vocation,

That You may grant us good priests and Bishops,

That You may give us good Christian families,

That You may grant us a spiritual renewal of the Church,

That You may guide and console the Holy Father,

Lamb of God, You take away the sins of the world; *spare us, O Lord.*

Lamb of God, You take away the sins of the world; *graciously hear us, O Lord.*

*__**We beseech You, hear us__ is repeated after each invocation.*

Lamb of God, You take away the sins of the world; *have mercy on us.*
Holy Spirit, hear us.
Holy Spirit, graciously hear us.
Lord, have mercy.

Christ, have mercy.
Lord, have mercy.
℣. Create a clean heart in us.
℟. *Renew a right spirit in us.*

Let us pray.
O merciful Father,
grant that Your Divine Spirit may cleanse,
inflame, and enlighten our minds and hearts.
Enable us to be fruitful in good works
for the glory of Your Majesty
and the spiritual and material well-being of all people.
We ask this through Jesus Christ Your Son
and the Holy Spirit.

Invocations to God the Holy Spirit

O Divine Spirit, Who have so often enlightened my soul
with the light of Your beams,
I thank You with all my heart.
O Divine Spirit, Who have sent me
so many holy inspirations and good desires,*
O Divine Spirit, Who sustain my weakness
by Your sovereign virtue,*
For the acts of virtue that You have made me accomplish
and that are due to Your salutary assistance,*
For the little good that I have been able to do by Your help,*

Archconfraternity Prayer
to the Holy Spirit

Holy Spirit, Lord of Light,
from Your clear celestial height,
Your pure beaming radiance give.

Come, O Father of the Poor,
come with treasures that endure,
come, O Light of all that live.

You of all Consolers best,
and the soul's delightsome Guest,
do refreshing Peace bestow.

You in toil are Comfort sweet,
pleasant Coolness in the heat,
solace in the midst of woe.

Light immortal, Light Divine,
visit now this heart of mine,
and my inmost being fill.

If You take Your grace away,
nothing pure in men will stay,
all their good is turned to ill.

Heal our wounds, our strength renew,
on our dryness pour Your dew,
wash the stains of guilt away.

Bend the stubborn heart and will,
melt the frozen, warm the chill,
guide the steps that go astray.

On all those who evermore
You confess and You adore,
in Your *Sevenfold Gifts* descend.

Give them *Comfort* when they die.
Give them Life with You on high,
give them Joys that never end.

Prayer of Consecration to the Holy Spirit

Before the multitude of heavenly witnesses,
I offer myself, soul and body,
to You, eternal Spirit of God.
I adore the brightness of Your purity,
the unerring keenness of Your justice,
and the power of Your love.
You are the strength and light of my soul.
In You I live and move and have my being.

I desire never to grieve You by infidelity to
    Your grace,
and I pray wholeheartedly to be preserved
from the slightest sin against You.
Make me faithful in my every thought,
and grant that I may always listen to Your
    voice,
watch for Your light,
and follow Your gracious inspirations.
I cling to You,
and beg You, in Your compassion,
to watch over me in my weakness.

Holding the pierced feet of Jesus,
gazing at His five wounds,
trusting in His Precious Blood,
and adoring His open side and stricken Heart,
I implore You, adorable Spirit,

so to keep me in Your grace
that I may never sin against You.
Grant me the grace,
O Holy Spirit of the Father and the Son,
to say to You always and everywhere:
"Speak, Lord, for Your servant is listening."

Prayer to the Spirit
for Universal Renewal

Holy Spirit,
fulfill in us the work begun by Jesus.
Let our prayer on behalf of the whole world
be fruitful and unwavering.
Hasten the time when each of us
will attain a genuine spiritual life.

Enliven our work
that it may reach all human beings,
all who have been redeemed by the Blood of
    Christ
and all His inheritance.

Take away our natural presumption
and uplift us with a holy humility,
with reverence for God
and selfless courage.

Let no vain attachment
impede the work of our state in life,
nor personal interest
divert us from the demands of justice.

May no scheming on our part
reduce love to our own petty dimensions.

May all be noble in us:
the quest and the respect for truth,
and the willingness to sacrifice
even to the cross and death.

And may all be accomplished
in accord with the final prayer
of the Son
to His heavenly Father
and in accord with the grace
that Father and Son give
through You, the Spirit of love,
to the Church and to its institutions,
to every soul and to all peoples.   Pope John XXIII

Novena Prayer to the Holy Spirit

H oly Spirit,
Third Person of the Blessed Trinity,
Spirit of truth, love, and holiness,
proceeding from the Father and the Son,
and equal to them in all things,
I adore You and love You with all my heart.

Dearest Holy Spirit,
confiding in Your deep, personal love for me,
I am making this novena for the following re-
      quest,
if it should be Your Will to grant it:
(Mention your request).

Teach me, Divine Spirit,
to know and seek my last end;

infuse in me the holy fear of God;
grant me true contrition and patience.
Do not let me fall into sin.
Give me an increase of faith, hope, and charity,
and bring forth in my soul all the virtues
proper to my state of life.

Make me a faithful disciple of Jesus
and an obedient child of the Church.
Give me efficacious grace
sufficient to keep the Commandments
and to receive the Sacraments worthily.
Give me the four Cardinal Virtues,
Your seven Gifts, and Your twelve Fruits.
Raise me to perfection in the state of life
to which You have called me
and lead me through a happy death
to everlasting life.
I ask this through Christ our Lord.

Short Invocations to the Holy Spirit

Holy Spirit, Spirit of truth,
come into our hearts;
shed the brightness of Your light upon the nations,
so that they may please You in unity of faith.

* * *

Holy Spirit,
Divine Guest of my soul,
abide in me
and grant that I may abide in You.

MARY—MOTHER, QUEEN, AND MEDIATRIX

Of all the Saints, Mary the Mother of our Lord is by far the favorite of all Christians. She has been invoked throughout the centuries by all classes of Christians for all types of requests, and her clients have invariably been heard. Her intercession with her Son began at the Marriage Feast of Cana and continues to this day from her heavenly seat.

PRAYERS TO THE BLESSED VIRGIN MARY

In a magnificent Apostolic Exhortation of February 2, 1974, Pope Paul VI set down the basis for prayer to Mary:

"The Church's norm of faith requires that her norm of prayer should everywhere blossom forth with regard to the Mother of Christ. Such devotion to the Blessed Virgin is firmly rooted in the revealed Word and has solid dogmatic foundations. It is based on the singular dignity of Mary, Mother of the Son of God, and therefore beloved Daughter of the Father and Temple of the Holy Spirit—Mary, who, because of this extraordinary grace, is far greater than any other creature on earth or in heaven" (Devotion to the Blessed Virgin Mary, *no. 56).*

The Bishops of the United States gave further details in a splendid Pastoral Letter of November 21, 1973:

"When Mary is honored, her Son is duly acknowledged, loved, and glorified, and His Commandments are observed. To venerate Mary correctly means to acknowledge her Son, for she is the Mother of God. To love her means to love Jesus, for she is always the Mother of Jesus.

"To pray to our Lady means not to substitute her for Christ, but to glorify her Son Who desires us to have loving confidence in His Saints, especially in His Mother. To imitate the 'faithful Virgin' means to keep her Son's Commandments" (Behold Your Mother, *no. 82).*

The prayers in this section are intended to help us pray to Mary in the way the Church wants: in line with the Bible, in harmony with the Liturgy, in an ecumenical spirit, and in accord with the latest anthropological studies. (See Paul VI, Devotion . . . , nos. 29-39.)

(We might point out that, besides the special prayers found in this section, we can also make use of any of the prayers to the Blessed Virgin Mary in the section "Official Prayers of the Church," pp. 37-49.)

TRADITIONAL PRAYERS

Hail Mary
(Ave Maria)

Hail Mary,
full of grace,
the Lord is with you.
Blessed are you among women
and blessed is the fruit of your womb, Jesus.

Holy Mary,
Mother of God,
pray for us sinners,
now and at the hour of our death.

We Fly to Your Patronage
(Sub Tuum)

We fly to your patronage,
O holy Mother of God;
despise not our petitions
in our necessities,
but deliver us always from all dangers,
O glorious and blessed Virgin.

Mary, Mother of Grace

Mary, Mother of grace,
Mother of mercy,
shield me from the enemy
and receive me at the hour of my death.

Remember, O Most Gracious Virgin Mary
(Memorare)

Remember, O most gracious Virgin Mary,
that never was it known
that anyone who fled to your protection,
implored your help or sought your intercession,
was left unaided.
Inspired with this confidence,
I fly to you, O Virgin of virgins, my Mother;
to you do I come,
before you I stand, sinful and sorrowful.
O Mother of the Word Incarnate,
despise not my petitions,
but in your mercy hear and answer me.

Hail, Holy Queen
(Salve Regina)

Hail, holy Queen, Mother of mercy,
hail, our life, our sweetness, and our hope.
To You do we cry,
poor banished children of Eve.
To you do we send up our sighs,
mourning and weeping in this valley of tears.

Turn then, most gracious Advocate,
your eyes of mercy toward us.
And after this our exile
show unto us the blessed fruit of your womb,
    Jesus.
O clement, O loving, O sweet Virgin Mary.

Prayer of Consecration to Mary

O my Queen and Mother,
I give myself entirely to you.
To show my devotion to you
I consecrate to you this day
my eyes, ears, mouth, heart,
and whole being without reserve.

Therefore, good Mother,
since I am your own,
keep me and guard me
as your property and possession.

The Angel of the Lord

(Angelus Domini)

a) *During the year* (outside of the Easter Season)

℣. **The Angel of the Lord declared unto Mary,**
℟. *And she conceived of the Holy Spirit.*

Hail Mary.

℣. **Behold the handmaid of the Lord,**
℟. *Be it done unto me according to your word.*

Hail Mary.

℣. **And the Word was made flesh,**
℟. *And dwelt among us.*

Hail Mary.

℣. Pray for us, O holy Mother of God,
℟. *That we may be made worthy of the promises of Christ.*

Let us pray.
Pour forth, we beg You, O Lord,
Your grace into our hearts:
that we, to whom the Incarnation of Christ Your Son
was made known by the message of an Angel,
may by His Passion and Cross
be brought to the glory of His Resurrection.
Through the same Christ our Lord.

Queen of Heaven

(Regina Caeli)

b) During the Easter Season

Queen of Heaven, rejoice, alleluia:
For He Whom you merited to bear, alleluia,
Has risen, as He said, alleluia.
Pray for us to God, alleluia.
℣. Rejoice and be glad, O Virgin Mary, alleluia.
℟. *Because the Lord is truly risen, alleluia.*

Let us pray.
O God, Who by the Resurrection of Your Son, our Lord Jesus Christ,
granted joy to the whole world:
grant, we beg You,
that through the intercession of the Virgin Mary, His Mother,
we may lay hold of the joys of eternal life.
Through the same Christ our Lord.

Holy Mary, Help the Helpless

Holy Mary,
help the helpless,
strengthen the fearful,
comfort the sorrowful,
pray for the people,
plead for the clergy,
intercede for all women consecrated to God;
may all who keep your sacred commemoration
experience the might of your assistance.

Prayer of Praise—Inviolata

O Mary,
you are inviolate,
pure and without stain,
you who became the glistening gate of heaven.
O most dear and gracious Mother of Jesus,
receive our modest songs of praise.

We beg you with heart and lips:
make our bodies and souls pure.
By your sweet prayers,
obtain eternal pardon for us.
O Mother most kind! O Queen! O Mary!
who alone remained inviolate!

At the Cross Her Station Keeping
(Stabat Mater)

At the Cross her station keeping,
Stood the mournful Mother weeping,
Close to Jesus to the last.

Through her heart, His sorrow sharing,
All His bitter anguish bearing,
Lo, the piercing sword has passed!

O, how sad and sore distressed
Was that Mother highly blessed
Of the sole-begotten One.
Christ above in torment hangs,
She beneath beholds the pangs
Of her dying glorious Son.

Is there one who would not weep
'Whelmed in miseries so deep
Christ's dear Mother to behold?
Can the human heart refrain
From partaking in the pain,
In that Mother's pain untold?

Bruised, derided, cursed, defiled,
She beheld her tender Child,
All with bloody scourges rent.
For the sins of His own nation
Saw Him hang in desolation
Till His Spirit forth He sent.

O sweet Mother! fount of love,
Touch my spirit from above,
Make my heart with yours accord.
Make me feel as you have felt.
Make my soul to glow and melt
With the love of Christ, my Lord.

Holy Mother, pierce me through.
In my heart each wound renew
Of my Savior crucified.

Let me share with you His pain,
Who for all our sins was slain,
Who for me in torments died.

Let me mingle tears with you
Mourning Him Who mourned for me,
All the days that I may live.
By the Cross with you to stay,
There with you to weep and pray,
Is all I ask of you to give.

Virgin of all virgins blest!
Listen to my fond request:
Let me share your grief Divine.
Let me, to my latest breath,
In my body bear the Death
Of your dying Son Divine.

Wounded with His every wound,
Steep my soul till it has swooned
In His very Blood away.
Be to me, O Virgin, nigh,
Lest in flames I burn and die,
In His awe-full judgment day.

Christ, when You shall call me hence,
Be Your Mother my defense,
Be Your Cross my victory.
While my body here decays,
May my soul Your goodness praise,
Safe in heaven eternally.
Amen. Alleluia.

Sequence for Mass of Our Lady of Sorrows

Prayer of Veneration

Holiest Virgin,
with all my heart I venerate you
above all the Angels and Saints in Paradise
as the Daughter of the Eternal Father,
and I consecrate to you
my soul with all its powers.

Hail Mary

Holiest Virgin,
with all my heart I venerate you
above all the Angels and Saints in Paradise
as the Mother of the only-begotten Son,
and I consecrate to you
my body with all its senses.

Hail Mary

Holiest Virgin,
with all my heart I venerate you
above all the Angels and Saints in Paradise
as the beloved Spouse of the Holy Spirit,
and I consecrate to you
my heart and all its affections,
praying you to obtain for me from the Most
    Holy Trinity
all the graces I need for my salvation.

Hail Mary

Prayer for the Grace To Love Jesus

Mary, my dear Mother,
how much I love you—
and yet in reality how little!
You teach me what I should know,

for you instruct me in
what Jesus is for me
and what I should be for Him.

O my beloved Mother,
how close to God you are,
and how completely filled with Him!
To the extent that we know God,
we are reminded of you.

Mother of God,
obtain for me the grace of loving my Jesus
and the grace of loving you.

Prayer To See Jesus through Mary

Most holy and immaculate Virgin,
my Mother:
you are the Mother of my Lord,
the Queen of the universe,
the advocate, hope, and refuge of sinners.

I, the most miserable of sinners,
have recourse to you today.
I venerate you, great Queen,
and I thank you for the many graces
you have bestowed on me until now.
I thank you especially for having saved me
    from hell,
which I have so often deserved by my many
    sins.

Most lovable Lady,
I love you,
and by the love I have for you

I promise to serve you always
and to do all I can to make you loved by others.
I place in you all my hope of salvation.
Mother of mercy,
receive me as your servant
and cover me with the mantle of your protec-
    tion.
Since you are so powerful with God,
deliver me from all temptations
or rather obtain for me the grace
to overcome them until death.

I ask of you a true love for Jesus Christ.
Through you I hope to die a good death.
My dear Mother,
by the love you have for almighty God
I beg you to help me always
and especially at the last moment of my life.
Do not leave me until you see me safe in
    heaven,
where I hope to thank and praise you forever.

Prayer of Dedication to Mary

Virgin full of goodness,
Mother of mercy,
I entrust to you my body and my soul,
my thoughts and my actions,
my life and my death.

O my Queen,
come to my aid
and deliver me from the snares of the devil.

Obtain for me the grace of loving
my Lord Jesus Christ, your Son,
with a true and perfect love,
and after Him, O Mary,
of loving you with all my heart
and above all things.

Litany of Loreto

Lord, have mercy.
Christ, have mercy.
Lord, have mercy.
Christ, hear us.
Christ, graciously hear us,
God, the Father of heaven,
  have mercy on us.
God the Son, Redeemer of
  the world,
  have mercy on us.
God, the Holy Spirit,
  have mercy on us.
Holy Trinity, one God,
  have mercy on us.
Holy Mary, *pray for us.* *
Holy Mother of God,
Holy Virgin of virgins,
Mother of Christ,
Mother of the Church,
Mother of Divine grace,
Mother most pure,
Mother most chaste,
Mother inviolate,
Mother undefiled,
Mother most amiable,
Mother most admirable,
Mother of good counsel,

Mother of our Creator,
Mother of our Savior,
Virgin most prudent,
Virgin most venerable,
Virgin most renowned,
Virgin most powerful,
Virgin most merciful,
Virgin most faithful,
Mirror of justice,
Seat of wisdom,
Cause of our joy,
Spiritual vessel,
Vessel of honor,
Singular vessel of devotion,
Mystical rose,
Tower of David,
Tower of ivory,
House of gold,
Ark of the covenant,
Gate of heaven,
Morning star,
Health of the sick,
Refuge of sinners,
Comforter of the afflicted,
Help of Christians,
Queen of Angels,
Queen of Patriarchs,

* *Pray for us* is repeated after each invocation.

Queen of Prophets,
Queen of Apostles,
Queen of Martyrs,
Queen of Confessors,
Queen of Virgins,
Queen of all Saints,
Queen conceived without original sin,
Queen assumed into heaven,
Queen of the most holy Rosary,
Queen of families,
Queen of peace,

Lamb of God, You take away the sins of the world; *spare us, O Lord!*
Lamb of God, You take away the sins of the world; *graciously hear us, O Lord!*
Lamb of God, You take away the sins of the world; *have mercy on us.*

℣. Pray for us, O holy Mother of God.
℟. *That we may be made worthy of the promises of Christ.*

Let us pray.
Grant, we beg You, O Lord God,
that we Your servants
may enjoy lasting health of mind and body,
and by the glorious intercession
of the Blessed Mary, ever Virgin,
be delivered from present sorrow
and enter into the joy of eternal happiness.
Through Christ our Lord.

Novena Prayer to Mary

I greet you,
ever-blessed Virgin, Mother of God,
throne of grace, and miracle of almighty power!
I greet you,
sanctuary of the Most Holy Trinity
and Queen of the Universe,

Mother of Mercy and Refuge of Sinners!
Most loving Mother,
attracted by your beauty and sweetness,
and by your tender compassion,
I confidently turn to you,
and beg you to obtain for me from your dear
Son
the favor I request in this novena:
(Mention your request).

Obtain for me also,
Queen of heaven,
the most lively contrition for my many sins
and the grace to imitate closely
those virtues that you practiced so faithfully,
especially humility, purity, and obedience.
Above all, I beg you
to be my mother and protectress,
to receive me into the number
of your devoted children,
and to guide me from your throne of glory on
high.

Do not reject my petitions,
Mother of Mercy!
Have pity on me,
and do not abandon me during life
or at the moment of my death.

Daughter of the Eternal Father,
Mother of the Eternal Son,
Spouse of the Holy Spirit,
Temple of the Adorable Trinity,
pray for me.

Immaculate and tender Heart of Mary,
refuge of the needy and hope of sinners,
filled with lively respect, love, and gratitude,
I devote myself forever to your service,
and I offer you my heart
with all that I am and all that is mine.

Accept this offering,
sweet Queen of Heaven and Earth,
and obtain for me,
from your dear Son, Jesus Christ,
the favor I ask, through your intercession,
in this novena.

Obtain for me also
a generous, constant love of God,
perfect submission to His holy Will,
the true spirit of a Christian,
and the grace of final perseverance.

CONTEMPORARY PRAYERS

Biblical Litany of Our Lady

Greeted by the angel Gabriel: Lk 1:28.
Full of Grace: *ibid.*
Mother of Jesus: Lk 1:31.
Mother of the Son of the Most High: Lk 1:32.
Mother of the Son of David: *ibid.*
Mother of the King of Israel: Lk 1:33.
Mother by act of the Holy Spirit: Lk 1:35; Mt 1:20.
Handmaid of the Lord: Lk 1:38.

Virgin, Mother of Emmanuel: Mt 1:23, citing Is 7:14; cf. Mt 5:2.

You in whom the Word became flesh: Jn 1:14.

You in whom the Word dwelt among us: *ibid.*

Blessed among all women: Lk 1:41; cf. Jdt 13:18.

Mother of the Lord: Lk 1:43.

Happy are you who have believed in the words uttered by the Lord: Lk 1:43.

Lowly handmaid of the Lord: Lk 1:48.

Called blessed by all generations: *ibid.*

You in whom the Almighty worked wonders: *ibid.*

Heiress of the promises made to Abraham: Lk 1:55.

Mother of the new Isaac: Lk 1:37 (Gn 18:14).

You who gave birth to your firstborn at Bethlehem: Lk 2:7.

You who wrapped your Child in swaddling clothes and laid Him in a manger: *ibid.*

Woman from whom Jesus was born: Gal 4:4; Mt 1:16, 21.

Mother of the Savior: Lk 2:11; Mt 1:21.

Mother of the Messiah: Lk 2:11; Mt 1:16.

You who were found by the shepherds with Joseph and the newborn Child: Lk 2:16.

You who kept and meditated on all things in your heart: Lk 2:19.

You who offered Jesus in the Temple: Lk 2:22.

You who put Jesus into the arms of Simeon: Lk 2:28.

You who marveled at what was said of Jesus: Lk 2:33.

You whose soul a sword should pierce: Lk 2:35.

Mother who were found together with the Child by the Wise Men: Mt 2:11.

Mother whom Joseph took into refuge in Egypt: Mt 2:14.

You who took the Child Jesus to Jerusalem for the Passover: Lk 2:42.

You who searched for Jesus for three days: Lk 2:46.

You who found Jesus again in His Father's house: Lk 2:46-49.

Mother whom Jesus obeyed at Nazareth: Lk 2:51.

Model of widows: cf. Mk 6:3.

Jesus' companion at the marriage feast at Cana: Jn 2:1-2.

You who told the servants, "Do as He shall tell you": Jn 2:5.

You who gave rise to Jesus' first miracle: Jn 2:11.

Mother of Jesus for having done the Will of the Father in heaven: Mt 12:50.

Mary who chose the better part: Lk 10:42.

Blessed for having heard the Word of God and kept it: Lk 11:28.

Mother standing at the foot of the Cross: Jn 19:25.

Mother of the disciple whom Jesus loved: Jn 19:26-27.

Queen of the Apostles, persevering in prayer with them: Acts 1:14.

Woman clothed with the sun: Rv 12:1.

Woman crowned with twelve stars: *ibid.*
Sorrowful Mother of the Church: Rv 12:2.
Glorious Mother of the Messiah: Rv 12:5.
Image of the new Jerusalem: Rv 21:2.
River of living water, flowing from the throne of
    God and the Lamb: Rv 22:1. Cf. Ps 45:5.

Prayer to Mary, Mother of the Church

O Blessed Virgin Mary,
the basic reason why you are Mother of the
    Church
is that you are the Mother of God
and the associate of Christ in His saving work.
Another reason is that you shine as the model
    of virtues
for the whole community of the elect.
You exemplified in your own life
the beatitudes preached by your Divine Son.
Hence, you are the perfect model
for the imitation of Christ
on the part of all human beings.

Obtain for us the graces we need
to follow your example.
Teach us to practice the beatitudes proper to
    our state
and to rejoice in being known as your children
who are members of the Church of God.
Let us work for the unity of the Church,
which your Son desired on earth
and which you now pray for in heaven.
Lead the whole human race

to acknowledge Christ Jesus, the one true Savior.
Drive from it all the calamities provoked by sin,
and bring it that peace which consists
in truth, justice, liberty, and love.

Prayer To Emulate Mary's Faith

Mary our Mother,
you consented in faith
to become the Mother of Jesus.
At the Angel's announcement
you received the Word of God in your heart
as well as in your body,
and you brought Life to the world.
You conceived in your heart, with your whole being,
before you conceived in your womb.

Obtain for us
a faith similar to your own,
which will enable us to hear the Word of God
and carry it out.
Let us imitate your Motherhood by our faith,
bringing Christ to birth in others
who have desperate need of Him.

Prayer to Mary Assumed into Heaven

O Blessed Virgin Mary,
united to the victorious Christ in heaven,

you are the image and first-flowering of the
    Church
as she is to be perfected in the world to come.
You shine forth as a sign of sure hope and so-
    lace
for the pilgrim People of God.
In your Assumption,
you manifest the fullness of Redemption
and appear as the spotless image of the Church
responding in joy to the invitation of the Bride-
    groom,
your Son,
Who is the firstfruits of those who have fallen
    asleep.

Grant that we may follow your example on
    earth
thereby imitating your Son as well
and being enabled to share your glory
with Him for all eternity.

Prayer to Mary, Queen of the Home

O Blessed Virgin Mary,
you are the Mother and Queen of every Chris-
    tian family.
When you conceived and gave birth to Jesus,
human motherhood reached its greatest
    achievement.
From the time of the Annunciation
you were the living chalice
of the Son of God made Man.
You are the Queen of the home.

As a woman of faith,
you inspire all mothers to transmit faith
to their children.

Watch over our families.
Let the children learn free and loving obedience
inspired by your obedience to God.
Let parents learn dedication and selflessness
based on your unselfish attitude.
Let all families honor you
and remain devoted to you
so that they may be held together
by your example and your intercession.

Prayer to Mary, Queen of the Universe

Mary, Queen of the Universe,
you are a Queen because you are the Mother of
the Word Incarnate.
Christ is universal King because He rules all
creatures
by His personal union with the Divinity.
He is King and you are Queen of all hearts.

Rule over us by the queenly power of your love
that the Kingdom of your Son—
the Kingdom of truth and life,
holiness and grace,
justice, love, and peace—
may come upon earth.
Grant grace to all people,
the Holy Spirit for the Church,
and peace for the whole world.

ADVENT-CHRISTMAS—GOD COMES TO US

The prayers of this time of year emphasize God's goodness in deciding to make Himself accessible to human beings, so that we might come to share in His life. They revolve around His Son Jesus Who became one of us by being born in a stable and leading a life of poverty and goodness.

PRAYERS IN ACCORD WITH THE LITURGICAL YEAR

PRAYERS FOR ADVENT - CHRISTMAS

The Second Vatican Council pointed out that "Liturgy is the summit toward which the activity of the Church is directed; at the same time it is the font from which all her power flows" (Constitution on the Sacred Liturgy, *no. 10*). *Accordingly, "prayers and devotions of the Christian people are to be so drawn up that they harmonize with the liturgical seasons, accord with the sacred Liturgy, are in some fashion derived from it, and lead the people to it"* (ibid., *no. 13*).

In other words, no private prayer is ever entirely estranged from liturgical prayer. The mystery of the Church is also the mystery of each believer. Baptized in the Spirit of Christ, we have been baptized in the Church and by the Church. The Church bears within herself the fullness of life and gives it to us. The Church continues the prayer of our Lord, and we pray in the Church.

The liturgical year is the periodic celebration of the Mystery of Christ; the community actualizes this Mystery, rendering it present through the liturgical actions. Thus while we "recall" the story of our salvation, we discover that we are involved in it—it is a story for today, one that concerns us.

Advent is the time of more than usual eager longing for Christ's coming in grace on Christmas Day while recalling His historical coming in the flesh and looking forward to His final coming in glory.

Christmas recalls Christ's visible coming into the world to bring light, life, and joy to a mankind lying in the darkness of ignorance and sin. It invites us to be born again through a more vital union with Jesus and to manifest Him to others.

ADVENT SEASON

Prayer for Enlightenment

O Lord,
in this time of Advent
help us to be aided by the Church
so that we will grasp the true meaning
of the perpetual longing
that lies at the heart of all people.
May we be aided in this quest
by the great figures of the Advent liturgy—
Mary Your Mother,
John Your Precursor,
and Isaiah Your Prophet.
Enable us to discover Whom and what we expect
and to be resolved to do whatever is needed
to have our expectation fulfilled.

Prayer To Hunger for Christ

O Lord,
enlighten our minds,
deliver us from all fear,
and make us totally open to Your grace.

Let us grasp the deep meaning of our existence
and of our lifelong hunger.
Help us to see that we hunger for You
Who are the living Bread
and the Fountain of perpetual life.
Aid us to overcome the desires
that may obscure this true hunger
so that we may run to meet You
as You come again
in Your grace
and in every person we encounter
along our life's journey to You.

Prayer of the Great "O" Antiphons

O Wisdom,
holy Word of God,
You rule all creation with power and true concern.
Come to teach us the way of salvation.

O sacred Lord,
and Leader of ancient Israel,
You communicated with Moses at the burning
bush
and gave him the law on Mount Sinai.
Come to set us free by Your mighty arm.

O Root of Jesse,
raised up as a sign of all peoples,
in Your presence kings become mute
and the nations worship before You.
Come to deliver us and do not delay.

O Key of David,
and Royal Power of Israel,
You open what no one can shut,
and You shut what no one can open.
Come and deliver Your people
imprisoned by darkness and the shadow of
    death.

O Radiant Dawn,
You are the Brightness of eternal light
and the Sun of justice.
Come to enlighten those who sit in darkness
and in the shadow of death.

O King of the Gentiles
and the longed-for Ruler of the nations,
You are the cornerstone Who make all one.
Come and save those whom You have created.

O Emmanuel,
our King and our Lawgiver,
You are the Desired of the nations
and the Savior of all people.
Come to save us, O Lord our God!

Prayer To Help Others Find Christ

O Lord Jesus,
I thank You for the gift of faith
and for the continual grace You give me
to nourish and strengthen it.
Enable me to cultivate the genuine desire for
    You
that lies beyond the zealous search

for justice, truth, love, and peace
found in our contemporaries.
Encourage these searchings, O Lord,
and grant that all true seekers
may look beyond the present moment
and catch sight of Your countenance in the
    world.
Come to the aid of those
who are weary and disillusioned
in their searching,
and inspire them with renewed hope
during this season of Christian hope.

Prayer for Christ's Triple Coming

Lamb of God,
You once came to rid the world of sin;
cleanse me now of every stain of sin.
Lord, You came to save what was lost;
come once again with Your salvific power
so that those You redeemed will not be pun-
    ished.
I have come to know You in faith;
may I have unending joy
when You come again in glory.

Prayer for Christ's Coming in Grace

O Lord Jesus,
during this Advent
come to us in Your grace.
Come to prepare our hearts, minds, and bodies
to welcome You on Christmas Day.

Come to comfort us in sadness,
to cheer us in loneliness,
to refresh us in weariness,
to buttress us in temptations,
to lead us in doubt,
and to exult with us in joy.

Prayer To Build Up the Body of Christ

O Lord Jesus,
sometimes I become impatient
while waiting for the coming of Your grace,
the coming of Your peace,
the coming of Your justice,
and the coming of Your love.
I forget that You also are waiting—
for my efforts
to build up Your Body in the world.

It is true, O Lord,
that unless You build the house
all who labor will come to nought.
But it is also true that
unless I join all people
in working for the coming of Your Kingdom,
that Kingdom of justice, love, and peace
will delay in coming.

Help me to realize
that You need my poor efforts,
and let me apply myself
with body, heart, and mind
to whatever task You may give me.

CHRISTMAS SEASON

Prayer To Begin a New Life

O Lord,
we desire to live the birth of Your Son
in all its truth and riches.
We want to welcome the God Who comes
to pitch His tent among us.
We wish to give thanks for so great a gift
and to begin a new life—
the life that You bestow on us
for our true happiness.

Help us to throw off all fear,
all laziness,
and all infidelity.
Everything is possible for us now,
since Jesus is born with and for us.

Prayer for Union with Christ

Lord Jesus,
open our hearts to Your renewed coming.
Help us to be conformed to You
in a new birth.
Cast out all fear,
which shuts us up within ourselves,
suffocates Your gifts,
and prevents You from working in us
Your perennial newness.

Grant that we may always discern Your com-
    ing
so that we may remain united with You
and work out our salvation
and the salvation of the world.

Prayer of Joy at the Birth of Jesus

Let the just rejoice,
for their Justifier is born.
Let the sick and infirm rejoice,
for their Savior is born.
Let captives rejoice,
for their Redeemer is born.
Let slaves rejoice,
for their Master is born.
Let free people rejoice,
for their Liberator is born.
Let all Christians rejoice,
for Jesus Christ is born.   St. Augustine of Hippo

Prayer to Jesus, God's Greatest Gift

O Jesus,
I believe that the greatest proof of God's love
is His gift to us of You,
His only Son.
All love tends to become like that which it
    loves.
You love human beings;
therefore You became Man.
Infinite love and mercy caused You,
the Second Person of the Blessed Trinity,

to leave the Kingdom of eternal bliss,
to descend from the throne of Your Majesty,
and to become a helpless Babe.
Eventually You even suffered and died
that we might live.

You wished to enter the world as a Child
in order to show that You were true Man.
But You become Man
also that man may become like God.
In exchange for the humanity that You take
      from us
You wish to make us share in Your Divinity
by sanctifying grace,
so that You may take sole possession of us.
Grant me the grace to love You in return
with a deep, personal, and productive love.

Prayer To Know and Love Jesus

My Lord Jesus,
I want to love You,
but You cannot trust me.
If You do not help me,
I will never do any good.
I do not know You;
I look for You but I do not find You.
Come to me, O Lord.
If I knew You,
I would also know myself.
If I have never loved You before,
I want to love You truly now.
I want to do Your Will alone;

putting no trust in myself,
I hope in You,
O Lord.

St. Philip Neri

Prayer for Christ's Rebirth in the Church

O Lord Jesus Christ,
we do not ask You to renew for us
Your birth according to the flesh.
We ask You
to incarnate in us Your invisible Divinity.
What You accomplished corporally in Mary
accomplish now spiritually in Your Church.
May the Church's sure faith conceive You,
her unstained intelligence give birth to You,
and her soul, united with the power of the
Most High,
preserve You forever.

Prayer That Christ May Be Known to All

O Lord,
give us a new Epiphany
when You will be manifested to the world:
to those who do not know You,
to those who do not want You,
to those who vilify Your Name,
to those who oppress Your Mystical Body,
to those who deny You,
and to all those who unconsciously long for
You.

Bring the day closer
when all people will know and love You
together with the Father
and the Holy Spirit—
and the Kingdom of God will have arrived.

Prayer to the Infant King

O Jesus,
the Magi offered You revealing gifts:
gold, because You are our King;
frankincense, because You are our God;
and myrrh, because You are our Redeemer.
Like the Magi,
I offer You my gifts:
the gold of my earnest love as Your faithful
subject;
the frankincense of frequent prayer as Your
creature;
and the myrrh of a generous self-sacrifice as a
sinner.

LENT-EASTER—WE ALL RISE IN JESUS

The prayers of this time of year stress penance (death to self with Christ) and joy (resurrection to a new person with Christ). They enable us to take a greater part in the Mystery of God's redeeming plan for the whole universe.

*C*hristians prepare themselves to celebrate the Paschal Mystery of our Lord's Death and Resurrection by a penitential season of forty days. Penance is the inner aversion to the evil existing in and around us and a generous conversion in love to God.

Traditionally the Lenten practices of prayer, almsgiving, and fasting were the means for achieving this aversion-conversion. And they are still valid when they are not seen as ends in themselves. But there are many other forms of penance that one may use—for example, working for social or individual justice, performing corporal and spiritual works of mercy, and a renewed interest in the Mysteries by which we are reborn to be children of God.

Easter is the highlight of all Christian celebrations. With Ascension-Pentecost as its completion, it lasts fifty days. Its lesson is that in Christ Who rose from the dead and ascended into glory all will be made to live. Through our Baptism, we now share in Christ's glorious Resurrection, but we will share it fully by partaking in His Ascension into heaven. The feast of Pentecost commemorates the outpouring of the pledge of our inheritance made to us at our Confirmation.

We should recall at this time of the year that we are an Easter people; hence we should also be a joyous people. Death (both spiritual and corporal) has lost its sting. There is no longer any reason for prolonged sadness at life's defeats or at the end of our earthly existence. United with Christ, we will live forever.

SEASON OF LENT

Prayer on the Beatitudes

O Lord Jesus, You said:
"Blessed are the poor in spirit,
for theirs is the Kingdom of heaven."
Keep us from being preoccupied with money
and worldly goods
and trying to increase them at the expense of
    justice.

O Lord Jesus, You said:
"Blessed are the gentle,
for they shall inherit the earth."
Help us not to be ruthless with one another,
and to eliminate the discord and violence
that exists in the world around us.

O Lord Jesus, You said:
"Blessed are those who mourn,
for they shall be comforted."
Let us not be impatient under our own burdens
and unconcerned about the burdens of others.

O Lord Jesus, You said:
"Blessed are those who hunger and thirst for
    justice,
for they shall be filled."
Make us thirst for You,
the Fountain of all holiness,
and actively spread Your influence
in our private lives and in society.

O Lord Jesus, You said:
"Blessed are the merciful,

for they shall receive mercy."
Grant that we may be quick to forgive
and slow to condemn.

O Lord Jesus, You said:
"Blessed are the clean of heart,
for they shall see God."
Free us from our senses and our evil desires,
and fix our eyes on You.

O Lord Jesus, You said:
"Blessed are the peacemakers,
for they shall be called children of God."
Aid us to make peace in our families,
in our country, and in the world.

O Lord Jesus, You said:
"Blessed are those who are persecuted
for the sake of justice,
for the Kingdom of heaven is theirs."
Make us willing to suffer for the sake of right
rather than to practice injustice;
and do not let us discriminate against our
     neighbors
or oppress and persecute them.

Prayer To Follow Christ

O Lord Jesus,
gentle and humble of Heart,
full of compassion and maker of peace,
You lived in poverty
and suffered persecution for the cause of jus-
     tice.

You chose the Cross as the path to glory
to show us the way of salvation.
May we receive the word of the Gospel joyfully
and live by Your example
as heirs and citizens of Your Kingdom.

Prayer for Pardon

O Lord,
 the hour of Your favor draws near,
the day of Your mercy and our salvation—
when death was destroyed and eternal life
    began.
We acknowledge our sins,
and our offenses are always before us.
Blot out all our wrongdoings
and give us a new and steadfast spirit.
Restore us to Your friendship
and number us among the living
who share the joy of Your Son's risen life.

Prayer To Be Freed of the Seven Deadly Sins

O meek Savior and Prince of Peace,
implant in me the virtues
of gentleness and patience.
Let me curb the fury of *anger*
and restrain all resentment and impatience
so as to overcome evil with good,
attain Your peace,
and rejoice in Your love.

O Model of humility,
divest me of all *pride* and arrogance.
Let me acknowledge my weakness and sinfulness,
so that I may bear mockery and contempt
for Your sake
and esteem myself as lowly in Your sight.

O Teacher of abstinence,
help me to serve You rather than my appetites.
Keep me from *gluttony*—
the inordinate love of food and drink—
and let me hunger and thirst for Your justice.

O Lover of purity,
remove all *lust* from my heart,
so that I may serve You with a pure mind
and a chaste body.

O Father of the poor,
help me to avoid all *covetousness* for earthly
goods
and grant me a love for heavenly things.
Inspire me to give to the needy,
just as You gave Your life
that I might inherit eternal treasures.

O Exemplar of love,
keep me from all *envy* and ill-will.
Let the grace of Your love dwell in me
that I may rejoice in the happiness of others
and bewail their adversities.

O zealous Lover of souls,
keep me from all *sloth* of mind or body.

Inspire me with zeal for Your glory,
so that I may do all things for You
and in You.

Prayer of Contrition

Merciful Father,
I am guilty of sin.
I confess my sins before You
and I am sorry for them.
Your promises are just;
therefore I trust that You will forgive me my
    sins
and cleanse me from every stain of sin.
Jesus Himself is the propitiation
for my sins and those of the whole world.
I put my hope in His atonement.
May my sins be forgiven through His Name,
and in His Blood may my soul be made clean.

Prayer To Know Jesus Christ

O Lord Jesus,
like St. Paul,
may I count everything as loss
in comparison with the supreme advantage
of knowing You.
I want to know You
and what Your Passion and Resurrection can
    do.
I also want to share in Your sufferings
in the hope that if I resemble You in death

I may somehow attain to the resurrection
from the dead.

Give me grace to make every effort
to supplement faith with moral courage,
moral courage with knowledge,
knowledge with self-control,
self-control with patience,
patience with piety,
piety with brotherly affection,
and brotherly affection with love.
May these virtues keep me both active and
    fruitful
and bring me to the deep knowledge of You,
Lord Jesus Christ.

(Holy Thursday)

Prayer To Appreciate the Mass

O Lord Jesus,
in order that the merits of Your sacrifice
on the Cross
might be applied to every soul of all time,
You willed that it should be renewed
upon the altar.
At the Last Supper, You said:
"Do this in remembrance of Me."
By these words
You gave Your Apostles and their successors
the power to consecrate
and the command to do what You Yourself
    did.

I believe that the Mass is
both a sacrifice and a memorial—
reenacting Your Passion, Death, and Resurrection.
Help me to realize that the Mass
is the greatest gift of God to us
and our greatest gift to God.
At every Mass I attend
grant me the grace
to participate fully, actively, and consciously
so as to give the greatest glory to God
and achieve the highest benefits for myself,
my relatives, friends, and benefactors
as well as all humankind.

(Good Friday)

Prayer of Love for the Crucified Lord

O Jesus,
it is not the heavenly reward You have promised
that impels me to love You;
neither is it the threat of hell
that keeps me from offending You.

It is You, O Lord;
it is the sight of You
affixed to the Cross and suffering insults;
it is the sight of Your broken body,
as well as Your pains and Your Death.

There is nothing You can give me
to make me love You.

For even if there were no heaven and no hell
I would still love You as I do!

(Holy Saturday)

Prayer To Be Joined with Christ in Death

O Lord,
Your sorrowing Mother stood by Your Cross;
help us in our sorrows
to share Your sufferings.
Like the seed buried in the ground,
You have produced the harvest of eternal life
    for us;
make us always dead to sin and alive to God.
Shepherd of all,
in death You remained hidden from the world;
teach us to love our hidden spiritual life
with You and the Father.

In Your role as the new Adam,
You went down among the dead
to release all the just there since the beginning;
grant that all who are dead in sin
may hear Your voice and rise to new life.
Son of the living God,
You have allowed us through Baptism
to be buried with You;
grant that we may also rise with You in Bap-
    tism
and walk in newness of life.

EASTER SEASON

Prayer for the Fruits of Christ's Resurrection

God, the Father of lights,
You have glorified the world
by the light of the risen Christ.
Brighten our hearts today
with the light of Your faith.

Through Your risen Son
You opened the gate of eternal life
for all human beings.
Grant to us who work out our salvation daily
the hope of eternal life.

You accepted the sacrifice of Your Son
and raised Him from the dead.
Accept the offering of our work,
which we perform for Your glory
and the salvation of all people.

Open our minds and hearts
to our brothers and sisters.
Help us to love and serve one another.

Your Son rose to lift up the downtrodden,
comfort the sorrowful,
cure the sick,
and bring joy to the world.
Help all people to cast off sin and ignorance
and enjoy Your Son's Paschal Victory.

Prayer for the Easter Virtues

O Lord,
the Resurrection of Your Son
has given us new life and renewed hope.
Help us to live as new people
in pursuit of the Christian ideal.
Grant us the wisdom to know what we must
do,
the will to want to do it,
the courage to undertake it,
the perseverance to continue to do it,
and the strength to complete it.

Prayer in Praise of Christ's Humanity

O Risen Lord,
Your Body was part of Your power,
rather than You a part in its weakness.
For this reason You could not but rise again,
if You were to die—
because Your Body,
once taken by You,
never was or could be separated from You
even in the grave.

I keep Your most holy Body before me
as the pledge of my own resurrection.
Though I die,
as I certainly shall die,
it only means that my life is changed,
for I shall rise again.
Teach me so to live as one who believes

the great dignity and sanctity of the material
frame
in which I am lodged.

(Ascension)

Prayer To Live a Full Life

O Lord,
Your Ascension into heaven
marks the culmination of the Paschal Mystery,
and it contains an important teaching for us.
We may live life as an earthly reality
and develop our human potential to its fullest.
We may make use of the results of science
to achieve a better life on this planet.
But in our best moments
we know that there must be more than all of
this,
a transcending Reality.
As Christians, we know that this Reality
is Your loving Father
Who awaits us with You and the Holy Spirit.
Where You have gone,
we ultimately will come—if we are faithful.

Prayer To Do God's Will

God, our Father,
help us not to lose sight of heavenly realities
while we apply ourselves diligently
to the circumstances of our earthly lives.

Enable us to hear Your voice,
follow Your Will,
pursue Your purpose,
and accept Your judgments.
Help us to act to please You
rather than ourselves or others.
And after our earthly lives are over,
let us be united with Your Son
in the unity that You share with Him
and the Holy Spirit.

Prayer to Christ Ascended into Heaven

O Lord Jesus,
I adore You,
Son of Mary,
my Savior and my Brother,
for You are God.
I follow You in my thoughts,
O firstfruits of our race,
as I hope one day by Your grace
to follow You in my person
into heavenly glory.

In the meantime,
do not let me neglect the earthly task
that You have given me.
Let me labor diligently all my life
with a greater appreciation for the present.
Let me realize that only by accomplishing
true human fulfillment

can I attain Divine fulfillment
and ascend to You at the completion of my
work.

(Pentecost)

Prayer To Receive the Spirit

Holy Spirit,
powerful Consoler,
sacred Bond of the Father and the Son,
Hope of the afflicted,
descend into our hearts
and establish in them Your loving dominion.
Enkindle in our tepid souls
the fire of Your love,
so that we may be wholly subject to You.

Prayer for the Grace of the Spirit

Lord and vivifying Spirit,
You moved over the primeval waters.
Move our hearts to follow Your inspirations.

You led Your people out of bondage
and gave them the freedom of God's people.
Free us from the bondage of our sins.

You came upon the Virgin Mary
and enabled her to become the Mother of God.
Come upon us and make us children of God.

You raised Jesus from the dead
and manifested His Divine power and glory.

Infuse the Divine life of grace in us
and help us never to lose it.

You came down on the first Christians
in tongues of fire
to establish Your Church.
Help us to remain ever faithful members.

You came to renew the face of the earth.
Make us true witnesses to our faith
before the world.

Prayer for the Gifts of the Spirit

Holy Spirit, Sanctifier blest,
deign to grant us:
the gift of fear,
which makes us shun all sin;
the gift of piety,
which makes us respect and love
the Three Divine Persons,
our parents and children,
as is proper for true children of God;
the gift of knowledge,
which makes us judge eternal and temporal
things
as God judges them;
the gift of fortitude,
which makes us bear all hardships
for the love and greater glory of God;
the gift of counsel,
which makes us be guided, and guide others,

in the Way of Truth, of Christlike Life;
the gift of understanding,
which makes us penetrate deeply into
what You, Holy Spirit, have deigned to re-
      veal;
the gift of wisdom,
which makes us relish all that is right
and is in line with Eternal Wisdom.
This we ask You to grant us,
Gift of God Most High,
Who live in perfect unity of Love
with the Father and the Son.

Prayer to the Holy Spirit
for Spiritual Benefits

Holy Spirit of light and love,
You are the substantial love
of the Father and the Son;
hear my prayer.
Bounteous bestower of most precious gifts,
grant me a strong and living faith,
which makes me accept all revealed truths
and shape my conduct in accord with them.

Give me a most confident hope in all Divine
      promises,
which prompts me to abandon myself unre-
      servedly
to You and Your guidance.

Infuse into me a love of perfect goodwill,
which makes me accomplish God's Will in all
      things
and act according to God's least desires.
Make me love not only my friends but my ene-
      mies as well
in imitation of Jesus Christ
Who through You
offered Himself on the Cross
for all people.

Holy Spirit,
animate, inspire, and guide me,
and help me to be always
a true follower of You.

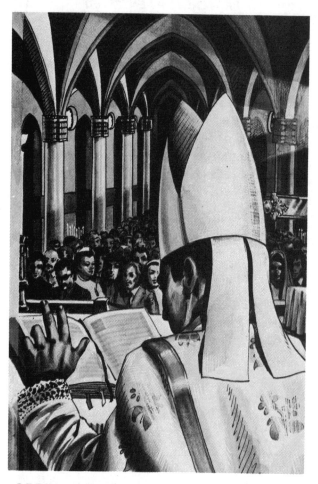

ORDINARY TIME—GROWTH IN THE SPIRIT

The prayers during this period stress growth, service, prayer, and God's Word. They enable us to work out our salvation through the Holy Spirit Who has been given us by Jesus and the Father.

174

PRAYERS FOR ORDINARY TIME

*O*rdinary Time is the name given to that part of the liturgical year which does not fall within one of the major seasons—Advent, Christmas, Lent, or Easter. During this season, the Church continues to celebrate the Lord's Resurrection—but in its application to our earthly lives.

This season numbers thirty-three or thirty-four weeks and is assigned to two parts of the year. The first part occurs from Epiphany to Lent and is concerned with the beginning of the Lord's preaching, His baptism, and His first manifestation.

The second part of the season occurs after Pentecost and runs to Advent. During this time the Church presents Jesus in His public ministry of healing and preaching.

Ordinary Time is a period of growth in the faith of all who follow the Liturgy. It is a time for the accentuation of the Christian virtues, prayer, ministry of service to others, and meditation on God's Word. The themes are endless. The sole unity is provided by the idea of spiritual growth symbolized by the green vestments that are worn.

During this time one may also concentrate on the major feasts that occur, such as the Trinity, Corpus Christi, Sacred Heart, Assumption, and Christ the King.

The following prayer services and individual prayers are only indicative. By a judicious use of the detailed Index, many more themes and prayers can be located and used.

Prayer of "Unprofitable" Servants

Lord, may we develop the earth
by the work of our minds and hands
and by the aid of technology,
so that it can bear fruit
and become a dwelling
worthy of the whole human family.

May we consciously take part in the life
of social groups,
so that we may carry out the design of God
on our behalf.

This design is that we should subdue the earth,
bring creation to perfection,
and develop ourselves to the full.
We will then be obeying the great Commandment
to place ourselves at the service of our brothers.

Some of us are also called to give witness
to the human desire for a heavenly home.
Others of us are called to dedicate ourselves
to the earthly service of others
and to make ready the material of the heavenly realm
by this ministry.

In both cases let us understand
that we are "unprofitable" servants.
We are simply doing what we must do,
and only with God's unfailing help.

Prayer for True Service

Heavenly Father,
help us to be true servants
after the example of Your Son.
Send forth Your Spirit
to give us a genuine spirit of service
of others.
Help us to realize that we are called
neither to run away from the world
nor to become slaves to its laws.
Rather our task is
to let ourselves be guided
by Your Spirit of love, freedom, and service.
In this way we will be able
to build fraternal and praying communities
at the very heart of the world.

Prayer To Learn How To Pray

Lord, You have fashioned us in such a way
that our lives are enriched by person-to-person
    contact.
Help us to realize that this applies to an en-
    counter
that may take place between us and You.

This encounter may take place through Bible
    reading,
a good sermon,
or the Eucharistic celebration.
But it may also take place

through contact with others
or through any event of our lives.

Most of all it may take place
through our prayer,
which is a dialogue
between us and You.
Through prayer we get to know You
and we also get to know ourselves.

Help us to learn how to pray—
by praying and by using formal prayers
as well as informal prayers.
Let us make use of communal prayer
as well as personal prayer.

Prayer for True Wisdom

O Heavenly Father,
every day of our lives
we are bombarded with words of wisdom
from all sides.
We are told how to do our job,
how to keep our health,
how to take our leisure,
how to attain happiness,
and how to live every aspect of our lives.
We are in desperate need
of maintaining our balance
amid the flow of such constant earthly wisdom.
Help us to measure everything against the wis-
    dom
of Your Son Jesus Christ.

Prayer To Take Hold of God's Word

The wisdom of Jesus is found in two main
    sources:
the Holy Bible
and the Sacred Tradition
of the Church.

But it can also reach us in hundreds of ways,
    such as:
encounters with other human beings,
meditation on good reading,
and the ordinary events of daily life.
The sole requirement is
that we be open to this wisdom.

The Bible is transmitted to us in human words
written in a time and culture different from
    our own.
It requires some effort on our part
so that it will be understood.

But if we persevere,
we will reach through the human word.
We will take hold of the Word of God,
which has the power to change the world
beginning with our own lives.

Prayer To Proclaim God's Word

Heavenly Father,
You have spoken to the world
through Your Prophets in ancient times
and then through Your only Son.

Your message is in the Scriptures
and Your Word is living and dynamic.
It is more penetrating than a two-edged sword,
reaching the very depths of human beings.
Help us to listen for Your Word
in the Bible,
in the Church,
and in the world.
Let us be transformed by its power
and bring it to others in our turn.

Prayer for a Productive Faith

O Lord,
increase my faith
and let it bear fruit in my life.
Let it bind me fast to other Christians
in the common certitude
that our Master is the God-Man
Who gave His life for all.
Let me listen in faith
to the Divine Word that challenges me.

Help me to strive wholeheartedly
under the promptings of my faith
in the building of a world ruled by love.
Enable me to walk in faith
toward the indescribable future
that You have promised
to all who possess a productive faith in You.

Prayer To Grow with the Church Year

O Lord Jesus,
I know that all human relations take time
if they are to grow and deepen.
This is also true of my relations
with You, the Father, and the Holy Spirit,
which must grow over the course of my life.
However, this growth is not automatic;
time alone means nothing
unless I add my earnest efforts to it.

You have inspired Your Church to set aside
        special times
when this growth can develop more intensely—
the special seasons of the Church year.
If I fail to move toward You during these times,
I waste precious opportunities
and endanger my spiritual life.
Help me to take them seriously
and make a real attempt to use them well,
so that I may grow into the person
You want me to be.

Prayer to Christ in the World

Lord Jesus,
let us realize
that every action of ours
no matter how small or how secular
enables us to be in touch with You.
Let our interest lie in created things—

but only in absolute dependence
upon Your presence in them.
Let us pursue You and You alone
through the reality of created things.
Let this be our prayer—
to become closer to You
by becoming more human.

Let us become a tree branch on the vine
that is You,
a branch that bears much fruit.
Let us accept You in our lives
in the way it pleases You to come into them:
as Truth, to be spoken,
as Life, to be lived,
as Light, to be lighted,
as Love, to be followed,
as Joy, to be given;
as Peace, to be spread about;
as Sacrifice, to be offered;
among our relatives and friends,
among our neighbors and all people.

Prayer for Hope amid Despair

O Lord,
the world we live in
is particularly plagued with the curse of despair.
We are confronted daily with countless rea-
    sons—
of a physical, mental, or technological nature—
that urge personal or communal despair.

It is only natural that there will be moments
when we are in danger of giving in to this de-
    spair.

At such times, let us look to You,
O Jesus,
as our light, guide, and exemplar,
as our sign of encouragement
on the journey to salvation.
You are the Lord of the world
and the goal of the universe
toward Whom everything and everyone is
    moving.
How then can we despair?
If You are with us, who is against us?
In You all problems can be worked out!

Prayer To Turn Authority into Service

Lord Jesus,
let me realize that authority is conferred on us
not for ourselves but for others—
it is not a privilege but a service.
More often than not
it consists in a call to suffering and trials.
A leader must bear the burdens of others
in order to be able to understand them
and to walk at their head—
as You did.

Help me to understand that
no matter what kind of authority we hold,
whether as parents and teachers over children,

or children over other children,
or workers over other workers,
it constitutes a share in Your own authority,
which is a duty of love and service.
Enable us to act on this knowledge
and turn our authority into service.

Prayer To Share Our Faith with Others

O Lord Jesus,
You manifested Yourself to the world
when You lived among human beings
in the days of Your earthly life.
Today, it is only through Your members—
such as myself—
that You are manifested to the world.
Help me to realize that we live in
what has aptly been termed a "global village,"
where all feel the need to share their experiences
and enrich one another.

In such a world
let me regard Your truth
not as something to be hoarded
but as something to be shared with others
by my actions as well as my words.
Help me to share my faith
with all whom I encounter—
not ostentatiously but quietly,
not with pride but with humility,
not out of fear but out of love,

not to overwhelm them but to inspire them,
not for my gain but for Your glory.

Prayer To Show True Hospitality
to Others

Lord Jesus,
help me to grasp the true notion of hospitality
and practice it toward others.
Most people are very willing
to welcome into their midst
their parents and friends
as well as those with whom
they have professional or social contacts.
But the Christian notion of hospitality
goes far beyond this
and is based on a supernatural attitude.
The welcome extended may be of a material
    nature,
called a corporal work of mercy;
or it may be of a spiritual nature,
called a spiritual work of mercy.

Lord,
never let me limit my welcome
only to those who can do the same for me.
Let me focus on the fact
that it is You Yourself that I welcome
when I show true hospitality to others,
especially those who are in need.
And a visit from You
is always a revelation of salvation.

Prayer To Be Generous in Giving

Lord Jesus,
You came to tell us
that the meaning of life consists in giving.
You told us that those who cling too tightly
to what they have—
without thought for others—
end up by losing everything.
You gave us new values
by which to measure the worth of a person's
life.

Help me to realize it is not
temporal success or riches or fame
that necessarily gives life meaning.
Rather it is the service rendered to others
in Your Name
that brings fulfillment
and makes my life worthwhile.
May all my activity help build God's Kingdom:
my suffering bear genuine fruit,
my obedience bring true freedom,
and my death lead to eternal life.

Prayer To Encounter God Frequently in Prayer

Heavenly Father,
let me realize that, like all prayer,
prayer of petition is primarily
a means of encountering You

and being sustained by You.
You know what we need
because You are a loving Father
Who watch over us at every moment.
Yet You respect our freedom
and wait for us to express our needs to You.

Let me have frequent recourse to You in prayer
so that I will purify my intentions
and bring my wishes into conformity with
        Your own.
Let me pray with fixed formulas
as well as in my own words—
whether they be long or short.
Above all, let me come before You
with a heart moved by Your Spirit
and a will ready to conform
to Your holy Will.

Prayer To Work and Pray
for Our Salvation

Heavenly Father,
while I wait patiently for the Day
when Jesus will return in my life,
help me to steer clear of two erroneous atti-
        tudes
in working out my salvation.
Let me avoid an abandonment to Your action
that will make me do nothing myself
and lead to the sin of presumption.

Let me also avoid a confidence in my own actions
that will make me do everything myself
and lead to the sin of despair when I fail.

Instead, let me blend these two attitudes:
praying as if everything depended on You
but working as if everything depended on
me.
In this way I will bear witness
that salvation comes from You
but requires our generous collaboration.

Prayer to Jesus the Final Word of God

O Lord Jesus,
You are the Word of God in human form
Who come to us at the end of a long dialogue
conducted by the Creator with His creatures.
You are God's final communication to us,
a communication in Word and Act.
The Word is the announcement
of the Good News of salvation
preached to the lowly and the sinful,
the Good News that is You Yourself.
The Act is Your Passion, which bears witness
that the Father loves us to the end,
that His Word is true and faithful,
and that all His promises are fulfilled in You.

Help us to receive this Word
at the hands of Your Church,
and let it awaken our faith

and explain our rites.
Most of all, let it give sight to our eyes,
enabling us to see all of life
with the eyes of God.

Prayer To Discern God's Call

Heavenly Father,
Your call never comes to us in a vacuum;
it comes to us in the circumstances
of our ordinary lives.
Therefore, our response cannot be given
only in the privacy of our own minds;
it must overflow into our daily lives.
You call us through our family,
through our community or Church,
and through the world.

Help me to see that when I say No
to the legitimate requests of my family,
my community, or my world,
I say No to You.
You have ordained that
whatever advances the true progress
of self,
of the Church,
and of the world
is my way of saying Yes to Your call.
May I take advantage of the daily opportunities
that You place at my disposal
to answer Your call affirmatively.

INDEX OF PRAYER THEMES

(Bold type indicates the main sections of the book and their divisions)